YA

Health Science Experiments

EXPERIMENTS FOR FUTURE SCIENTISTS

Health Science Experiments

Edited by **Aviva Ebner, Ph.D.**

CHELSEA HOUSE
An Infobase Learning Company

HEALTH SCIENCE EXPERIMENTS

Text and artwork copyright © 2011 by Infobase Learning

Chelsea House
An imprint of Infobase Learning
132 West 31st Street
New York NY 10001

Library of Congress Cataloging-in-Publication Data
Health science experiments/edited by Aviva Ebner.
    p.cm.—(Experiments for future scientists)
Includes bibliographical references and index.
ISBN 978-1-60413-853-5 (alk. paper)
1. Medicine—Juvenile literature. 2. Health—Juvenile literature. 3. Medicine—Biology literature.
I. Ebner, Aviva
R130.5.H436 2011
610—dc22
                                        2010029120

Chelsea House books are available at special discounts when purchased in bulk quantities for businesses, associations, institutions, or sales promotions. Please call our Special Sales Department in New York at (212) 967-8800 or (800) 322-8755.

You can find Chelsea House on the World Wide Web at http://www.chelseahouse.com

All links and Web addresses were checked and verified to be correct at the time of publication. Because of the dynamic nature of the Web, some addresses and links may have changed since publication and may no longer be valid.

Editor: Frank K. Darmstadt
Copy Editor for A Good Thing, Inc.: Milton Horowitz
Project Coordination: Aaron Richman
Art Director: Howard Petlack
Production: Shoshana Feinstein
Illustrations: Hadel Studios
Cover printed by: Yurchak Printing, Landisville, Pa.
Book printed and bound by: Yurchak Printing, Landisville, Pa.
Date printed: May 2011
Printed in the United States of America

10 9 8 7 6 5 4 3 2 1

This book is printed on acid-free paper.

Contents

Preface

Educational representatives from several states have been meeting to come to an agreement about common content standards. Because of the No Child Left Behind Act, there has been a huge push in each individual state to teach to the standards. Teacher preparation programs have been focusing on lesson plans that are standards-based. Teacher evaluations hinge on evidence of such instruction, and various districts have been discussing merit pay for teachers linked to standardized test scores.

The focus in education has shifted to academic content rather than to the learner. In the race to raise test scores, some schools no longer address all areas of a well-rounded education and have cut elective programs completely. Also, with "high-stakes" standardized testing, schools must demonstrate a constant increase in student achievement to avoid the risk of being taken over by another agency or labeled by it as failing. The appreciation of different talents among students is dwindling; a one-size-fits-all mentality has taken its place. While innovative educators struggle to teach the whole child and recognize that each student has his or her own strengths, teachers are still forced to teach to the test. Perhaps increasing test scores helps close the gap between schools. However, are we creating a generation of students not prepared for the variety of careers available to them? Many students have not had a fine-arts class, let alone been exposed to different fields in science. We *must* start using appropriate strategies for helping all students learn to the best of their abilities. The first step in doing this is igniting a spark of interest in a child.

Experiments for Future Scientists is a six-volume series designed to expose students to various fields of study in grades five to eight, which are the formative middle-school years when students are eager to explore the world around them. Each volume focuses on a different scientific discipline and alludes to possible careers or fields of study related to those disciplines. Each volume contains 20 experiments with a detailed introduction, a step-by-step experiment that can be done in a classroom or at home, thought-provoking questions, and suggested "Further Reading" sources to stimulate the eager student. Of course, "Safety Guidelines" are provided, as well as "Tips for Teachers" who implement the lessons. A "Scope and Sequence Chart" and lists for "Grade Level" and "Setting" help the teacher with alignment to content standards, while the experiments themselves help students and adults think outside the paradigm of typical activities used in most science programs.

Science is best learned by "doing." Hands-on activities and experiments are essential, not only for grasping the concepts but also for generating excitement in today's youth. In a world of video games, benchmark tests, and fewer course choices, the experiments in these books will bring student interest back to learning. The goal is to open a child's eyes to the wonders of science and perhaps imbue some "fun" that will inspire him or her to pursue a future in a field of science. Perhaps this series will inspire some students to become future scientists.

—Aviva Ebner, Ph.D.
Faculty, University of Phoenix Online and
Educational Consultant/Administrator K-12
Granada Hills, California

Acknowledgments

I thank the following people for their assistance and contributions to this book: Mindy Perris, science education expert, New York City Board of Education District 24, for her suggestions and samples of experiments; Janet Balekian, administrator/science educator of SIAtech schools in Los Angeles, for experiment suggestions; Boris Sinofsky, retired Los Angeles Unified School District science teacher and mentor, for his evaluation of experiments; Dr. Esther Sinofsky, Director of Instructional Media Services for Los Angeles Unified School District, for assisting with research; Michael Miller, educator, and Cassandra Ebner, college student, for their help with the glossary and index; Aaron Richman of A Good Thing, Inc., for his publishing services, along with Milton Horowitz for always providing support and a personal touch to any project; and Frank K. Darmstadt, executive editor, Chelsea House, for his consistent hard work and his confidence in me.

This book is dedicated to my husband, Mark, and my children, Cassandra (Cassie) and Brooke, for their patience in acting as "patients" in the name of testing science experiments.

Introduction

A wide variety of articles in major newspapers have declared it. Public service announcements have tried to create awareness of it. Parents do their best to deal with it. What is "it"? There is clearly a national health epidemic and it is not the latest strain of flu. "It" is the issue of childhood obesity.

Over decades, the national trend has been toward the "supersizing" of meals and creating convenience versus the serving of healthy foods. The results have been disastrous. The nation's average weight has risen, the number of obese children has increased dramatically, many children do not exercise, and the incidence of serious health conditions, such as diabetes, has skyrocketed. Conflicting messages appear in the media, barraging children with "role models" of excessively thin actors and actresses while at the same time selling high-calorie products.

The only way to turn the tide in this epidemic is through education and good choices. It is up to parents and teachers to educate children about how the choices they make impact their health both now and in the future. As children get older, they are faced with increasingly difficult choices through peer pressure. Without early guidance, we leave children ill prepared to deal with such prospects.

The July 26th issue of the *Modesto Bee* included "Yes, There Is a Free Lunch," a fascinating article about how schools are trying to become creative to educate youth about health and wellness. One district has actually taken to driving around an RV as a mobile nutritional center. A July 22nd editorial in *The Hill* contained "Kids' School Meals Need Day in Senate," an editorial that cited how educators are urging Congress to reauthorize child nutrition programs. On July 21st, *Pegasus News* announced that a Texas school district will eliminate foods high in sugar and reduce the offering of breaded and pre-fried foods. A recent issue of the National Academies Press included "The Intersection of Nutrition and Health," an article that shared some startling statistics, including the following: "Americans consume an average of more than 3,400 mg of sodium per day—well in excess of the maximum daily intake of 2,300 mg of sodium. Analysts estimate that population-wide reductions in sodium could prevent more than 100,000 deaths annually."

An even more disturbing fact is this: "About 68 percent of adults in the United States aged 20 years or older are either overweight or obese. Among children, the rate is nearly 32 percent." With these types of statistics, a few wellness programs can only make a small dent. It is imperative that health education starts at a young age and that continued interest in maintaining wellness be a priority for children.

Health education should also include self-esteem and self-concept, both of which are integral to emotional and mental health. *Health Science Experiments* includes activities that have children consider stress and self-concept, making them more aware of otherwise intangible topics. However, it is clear that emotional health has an impact on physical health. As they go hand in hand, one or the other cannot be ignored.

This volume was written with a dual purpose in mind—first and foremost, to provide engaging activities that will help children learn about health issues in a fun way so that these children will be inspired to make lifelong, healthy choices. The secondary purpose of this book is to introduce youth to various disciplines within the health science field, perhaps planting the seed in the mind of a child for considering a career in the health sciences.

After completing "Eating Healthy and Fitness Plan," "Healthy Food Choices," "Evaluating the Sugar Content of Popular Drinks," "Comparing Vitamin-C Content," and "Comparing Iron in Breakfast Cereals," students will be equipped to make healthy food choices and be aware of the different levels of nutrition found in foods. Furthermore, children will be equipped with knowledge for making good decisions about how they care for their bodies through "Tooth Care—Parts 1 and 2" and "Evaluating Stressors." They will learn the dangers of smoking and alcohol while completing "Simulating the Negative Effects of Tobacco—Parts 1 and 2" and "Modeling Blood Alcohol Content." Children will also learn to be more critical of advertising and to decide for themselves about the quality of a product in "Comparing Different Brands of Bottled Water" and "Studying Consumerism in TV Commercials." We can help teach children to prevent certain illnesses in "The Spread of Infection" and "Food Preservation." "Creating a Life Map" and "Self-Esteem" will provide children with insights into their self-concept and goals. Finally, "Taking Blood Pressure." "Studying Nerves—Sensitivity Training" and "Taking a Pulse at Multiple Sites" may inspire some young people to pursue study or a career in the health field.

Each experiment has a brief introduction to educate children about the health topic being discussed. Terms set in italics in these paragraphs are listed in the glossary. The "Observation" questions at the end of each experiment are intended to make children pause and think about the impact of their own wellness. In the "Further Reading" section of each experiment, suggestions for additional reading, both of books and the Internet, are recommended to help students pursue their interest in that topic. There is also an "Internet Resources" section at the back of this volume for even more recommendations.

Whether these experiments create awareness of health issues or spawn future nutritionists or doctors, students will enjoy this smorgasbord of health-related activities. After years of growing health issues in the United States, it is time to make sure that our children are well informed so that they can avoid the poor health practices that have been rampant in society and focus on a long and healthy life.

Safety Guidelines

REVIEW BEFORE STARTING ANY EXPERIMENT

Each experiment includes special safety precautions that are relevant to that particular project. These do not include all the basic safety precautions that are necessary whenever you are working on a scientific experiment. For this reason, it is absolutely necessary that you read and remain mindful of the General Safety Precautions that follow. Experimental science can be dangerous and good laboratory procedure always includes following basic safety rules. Things can happen quickly while you are performing an experiment—for example, materials can spill, break, or even catch on fire. There will not be time after the fact to protect yourself. Always prepare for unexpected dangers by following the basic safety guidelines during the entire experiment, whether or not something seems dangerous to you at a given moment.

We have been quite sparing in prescribing safety precautions for the individual experiments. For one reason, we want you to take very seriously the safety precautions that are printed in this book. If you see it written here, you can be sure that it is here because it is absolutely critical.

Read the safety precautions presented here and at the beginning of each experiment before performing each lab activity. It is difficult to remember a long set of general rules. By rereading these general precautions every time you set up an experiment, you will be reminding yourself that lab safety is critically important. In addition, use your good judgment and pay close attention when performing potentially dangerous procedures. Just because the book does not say "Be careful with hot liquids" or "Don't cut yourself with a knife" does not mean that you can be careless when boiling water or using a knife to punch holes in plastic bottles. Notes in the text are special precautions to which you must pay special attention.

GENERAL SAFETY PRECAUTIONS

Accidents can be caused by carelessness, haste, or insufficient knowledge. By practicing safety procedures and being alert while conducting experiments, you can avoid taking an unnecessary risk. Be sure to check the individual experiments in this book for additional safety regulations and adult supervision requirements. If you will be working in a laboratory, do not work alone. When you are working off site, keep in groups with a minimum of three students per group, and follow school rules and state legal requirements for the number of supervisors required. Ask an adult supervisor with basic training in first aid to carry a small first-aid kit. Make sure everyone knows where this person will be during the experiment.

PREPARING

- Clear all surfaces before beginning experiments.
- Read the entire experiment before you start.
- Know the hazards of the experiments and anticipate dangers.

PROTECTING YOURSELF

- Follow the directions step by step.
- Perform only one experiment at a time.
- Locate exits, fire blanket and extinguisher, master gas and electricity shut-offs, eyewash, and first-aid kit.
- Make sure there is adequate ventilation.
- Do not participate in horseplay.
- Do not wear open-toed shoes.
- Keep floor and workspace neat, clean, and dry.
- Clean up spills immediately.
- If glassware breaks, do not clean it up by yourself; ask for teacher assistance.
- Tie back long hair.
- Never eat, drink, or smoke in the laboratory or workspace.
- Do not eat or drink any substances tested unless expressly permitted to do so by a knowledgeable adult.

USING EQUIPMENT WITH CARE

- Set up apparatus far from the edge of the desk.
- Use knives or other sharp, pointed instruments with care.

- Pull plugs, not cords, when removing electrical plugs.
- Clean glassware before and after use.
- Check glassware for scratches, cracks, and sharp edges.
- Let your teacher know about broken glassware immediately.
- Do not use reflected sunlight to illuminate your microscope.
- Do not touch metal conductors.
- Take care when working with any form of electricity.
- Use alcohol-filled thermometers, not mercury-filled thermometers.

USING CHEMICALS

- Never taste or inhale chemicals.
- Label all bottles and apparatus containing chemicals.
- Read labels carefully.
- Avoid chemical contact with skin and eyes (wear safety glasses or goggles, lab apron, and gloves).
- Do not touch chemical solutions.
- Wash hands before and after using solutions.
- Wipe up spills thoroughly.

HEATING SUBSTANCES

- Wear safety glasses or goggles, apron, and gloves when heating materials.
- Keep your face away from test tubes and beakers.
- When heating substances in a test tube, avoid pointing the top of the test tube toward other people.
- Use test tubes, beakers, and other glassware made of Pyrex™ glass.
- Never leave apparatus unattended.
- Use safety tongs and heat-resistant gloves.
- If your laboratory does not have heatproof workbenches, put your Bunsen burner on a heatproof mat before lighting it.
- Take care when lighting your Bunsen burner; light it with the airhole closed and use a Bunsen burner lighter rather than wooden matches.

- Turn off hot plates, Bunsen burners, and gas when you are done.
- Keep flammable substances away from flames and other sources of heat.
- Have a fire extinguisher on hand.

FINISHING UP

- Thoroughly clean your work area and any glassware used.
- Wash your hands.
- Be careful not to return chemicals or contaminated reagents to the wrong containers.
- Do not dispose of materials in the sink unless instructed to do so.
- Clean up all residues and put in proper containers for disposal.
- Dispose of all chemicals according to all local, state, and federal laws.

BE SAFETY CONSCIOUS AT ALL TIMES!

1. EATING HEALTHY AND FITNESS PLAN

Introduction

One way to improve your health is to maintain an appropriate *Body Mass Index* (BMI). This can be achieved through proper *nutrition and exercise*. The BMI of children is somewhat different from that of adults as *bone density*, growth, and other issues are taken into consideration. There are online BMI calculators that provide an approximate BMI based on a person's height and weight. However, such calculators do not take into account the weight of muscle mass for athletes, as muscle weighs more than fat, producing a false high BMI number. A more accurate measurement of BMI requires special equipment that can differentiate between the weight of muscle and fat tissue, such as *calipers* for skin fold measurement and special tanks for weighing water.

In order to maintain a healthy BMI level, not only do you need to have a healthy diet but also you must exercise regularly. Everyone has his or her own *optimal* level of fitness, so physical fitness plans should be individualized for a person's needs.

In this activity, you will assess your BMI and fitness level, then use this information to create a personalized fitness plan for yourself.

Time Needed

about a week

What You Need

✎ computer with Internet access to review the following Web sites:
URL: http://apps.nccd.cdc.gov/dnpabmi/Calculator.aspx

URL: http://www.webmd.com/heart-disease/tc/interactive-tool-what-is-your-target-heart-rate-what-does-this-tool-measure

URL: http://www.healthstatus.com/calculate/cbc

URL: http://www.thecaloriecounter.com

- lined paper, a few sheets
- pen or pencil
- clock or watch with a seconds hand, or a stopwatch

Safety Precautions

Please review and follow the safety guidelines at the beginning of this volume. Always follow Internet safety guidelines. Adult supervision is recommended for Internet access and to oversee physical exercises. Weight and body image can be sensitive issues for children and teens; any personal information about a student should not be shared with others without the permission of his or her parents.

What You Do

1. Visit the Web site URL: http://apps.nccd.cdc.gov/dnpabmi/Calculator.aspx and follow the instructions to calculate your BMI.

2. Record your BMI.

3. Find your pulse on your neck or wrist (Figure 1).

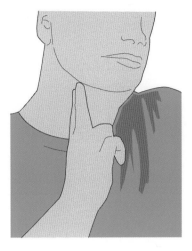

Finding pulse on neck   Finding pulse on wrist

Figure 1

4. Take your resting pulse for 1 minute and record your pulse rate.

5. Do jumping jacks for 60 seconds.

6. Find your pulse again and take your active pulse rate immediately following the jumping jacks.

7. Visit the Web site URL: http://www.webmd.com/heart-disease/tc/interactive-tool-what-is-your-target-heart-rate-what-does-this-tool-measure.

8. Determine your target heart rate.

9. Visit the Web site URL: http://www.healthstatus.com/calculate/cbc.

10. Key in the activities you typically do on a daily basis and determine how many calories you burn daily.

11. Keep a journal listing foods eaten for 7 days by using the template of the data table to track your food and calorie intake each day. Visit URL: http://www.thecaloriecounter.com/ if you do not know the calories of the item you have eaten.

12. Add up your calorie intake for each day.

13. Calculate the number of all the calories you have consumed in the course of a week and divide that number by 7 to find your average daily calorie intake.

Data Table	
Food eaten today (date)	Number of calories
1	
2	
3	
4	
5	
6	
7	
	Average daily calorie intake

 Observations

1. How did your BMI compare to the ranges for underweight, normal, and obese individuals?

2. How did your heart rate compare to your target heart rate?

3. Compare your calorie intake to calories burned on a daily basis. How do you think these comparisons affect your body? Are you burning off more calories than you eat, eating more calories than you burn, or maintaining a balance between calorie intake and calories burned?

4. Based on all the information you have collected, what plan do you have for your nutrition and fitness levels?

5. What or who are possible resources to assist you with creating a fitness plan?

Our Findings

Please refer to the Our Findings appendix at the back of this volume.

Further Reading

"Body Mass Index." *International Encyclopedia of the Social Sciences*. 2008. Available online. URL: http://www.encyclopedia.com/doc/1G2-3045300220.html. Accessed December 1, 2010. Explains what Body Mass Index is and its measure in terms of obesity.

"Calculate Your Body Mass Index." Department of Health and Human Services. Available online. URL: http://www.nhlbisupport.com/bmi/. Accessed December 1, 2010. Web site that provides a BMI calculator as well as links to information about controlling weight and assessing health risks.

Michaels, Jillian. *Winning by Losing: Drop the Weight, Change Your Life*. New York: Harper Paperbacks, 2007. From one of the personal trainers of the hit television show *The Biggest Loser*, this book serves as a guide to exercise and boosting metabolism.

"Physical Fitness." *The Columbia Encyclopedia,* 6th ed. 2008. Available online. URL: http://www.encyclopedia.com/doc/1E1-physfit.html. Accessed December 1, 2010. Brief article explaining the concept of being physically fit.

"You Can Learn a Lot From a Label." Nutrition Data. Available online. URL: http://www.nutritiondata.com/. Accessed December 1, 2010. Explanation on how to read the nutritional labels found on packaged food.

2. HEALTHY FOOD CHOICES

Introduction

The United States Department of Agriculture (USDA) provides dietary guidelines that take into account *exercise* recommendations, *nutritional* requirements, and scientific literature related to food and *nutrition*. New guidelines are then released about every 5 years. The official Web site of the USDA also provides the most updated *food pyramid* with recommendations for healthy eating of all of the *food groups*. However, preparing healthy food takes time, and we all seem to be leading busier and busier lives. Sometimes, it is more convenient to drive through a fast-food restaurant and order a tasty and reasonably priced meal. Fast food can be prepared and served quickly and allow the restaurant to keep costs low for consumers. Eating fast food, though, may not be eating healthy. In fact, most fast-food restaurants offer foods that are high in calories and fat.

In this activity, you will research some popular fast-food chains and compare the nutrition in their meals to the recommendations of the USDA. You will then make healthy food choices based on your research.

Time Needed

2 hours

What You Need

✎ computer with Internet access to review the following Web sites:

URL: http://www.usda.gov

URL: http://www.mcdonalds.com/usa/eat.html

URL: http://www.tacobell.com/nutrition/

URL: http://www.bk.com/en/us/menu-nutrition/category1/menu-item5/index.html

URL: http://www.wendys.com/food/NutritionLanding.jsp

- color printer and white paper or old magazines that can be cut up
- white poster board (any size)
- ruler
- pencil
- colored markers
- glue stick
- scissors

Safety Precautions

Please review and follow the safety guidelines at the beginning of this volume. Always follow Internet safety guidelines. Adult supervision is recommended for Internet access and to supervise the use of scissors.

What You Do

1. Using colored markers and poster board, title your poster "Healthy Food Choices" (Figure 1).

Healthy Food Choices

Figure 1

2. Divide the rest of your poster into a grid, 4 boxes across by 5 boxes down, using a ruler and a pencil (Figure 1).

3. In the first column, list fast-food chains, and write "USDA recommended" in the last box (Figure 2).

Healthy Food Choices			
McDonald's			
Taco Bell			
Burger King			
Wendy's			
USDA recommended			

Figure 2

4. Visit the first fast-food restaurant Web site listed in Figure 2 and select 3 popular food items or meals to represent breakfast, lunch, and dinner.

5. Research the nutritional value of those food items on the Web site.

6. Print out photos of the food items, or cut out comparable pictures from an old magazine that you have permission to cut.

7. Going across the row you have created on your poster for that fast-food chain, glue the photos for each meal into a different box on your grid (for examples, see the first column in Figure 3).

Healthy Food Choices			
McDonald's			
Taco Bell	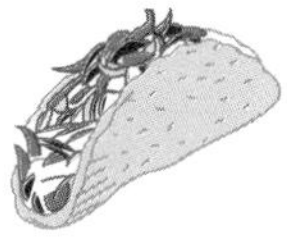		
Burger King	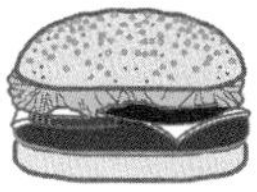		
Wendy's			
USDA recommended			

Figure 3

8. Next to each picture, list the nutritional information about that meal that you found on the Web site.

9. Repeat steps 4 to 8 with the other fast-food chain Web sites.

10. Now visit the USDA Web site (see page 6, under "What You Need").

11. Research what the USDA recommends for breakfast, lunch, and dinner.

12. Find pictures to print out, or cut out pictures from magazines of these foods.

13. Glue the pictures into the boxes of the grid in the row for USDA (Figure 3).

14. Write in the nutritional information next to each picture.

 **Observations**

1. Did any of the foods you selected from the fast-food chains match the USDA recommendations for nutrition? If so, which one and what was the meal?

2. Now that you are aware of the nutritional content of the food and what the USDA recommends, what menu items would you recommend to people who wanted to make healthy food choices at these restaurants?

3. How has this activity influenced your food choices? Why?

Our Findings

Please refer to the Our Findings appendix at the back of this volume.

Further Reading

Aldana, Steven. *Stop and Go Fast-food Nutrition Guide.* Mapleton, UT: Maple Mountain Press, 2007. A handbook with nutritional information for meals at fast-food chains.

Brownell, Kelly, and Katherine Battle Horgen. *Food Fight: The Inside Story of the Food Industry, America's Obesity Crisis, and What We Can Do About It.* New York: McGraw-Hill, 2004. Discusses how Americans have fallen into the fast-food habit and the long-term impact this has had on health.

Greene, Bob. *Get With the Program! Guide to Fast-Food and Family Restaurants.* New York: Simon & Schuster, 2003. A guide to eating healthy when eating out, this book assists people in making better food choices at fast-food restaurants.

Spurlock, Morgan. *Don't Eat This Book: Fast-Food and the Supersizing of America.* New York: Berkley Trade, 2006. Morgan Spurlock, producer and star of the movie *Supersize Me,* goes into details about the effects of fast food on health.

Super Size Me. Hulu.com. Available Online. URL: http://www.hulu.com/watch/63283/super-size-me. Accessed December 1, 2010. Web site that has access to free video of the movie *Super Size Me*, which details the health of a man who eats only fast food for 30 days.

3. SELF-ESTEEM

Introduction

Self-esteem is the realistic or favorable impression a person has of himself or herself. A person with high self-esteem typically has a healthy and positive view of self as opposed to someone with low esteem, who has an overall unrealistically negative *self-perception*. Low self-esteem can lead people to engage in such *risk behaviors* as illegal drug use, dangerous driving, fist fights, and similar types of actions. The first step in reinforcing self-esteem is to take a *personal inventory* of yourself and identify your strengths. A personal inventory is a series of questions that allow you to identify your likes and dislikes, as well as your strengths and weaknesses. By knowing who you are, your abilities, and your goals, you are better equipped to focus on *concrete* issues to maintain a positive outlook rather than becoming *pessimistic*.

In this activity, you will take a personal inventory to determine your strengths and weaknesses and create a project that reflects who you are.

Time Needed

1 to 2 hours

What You Need

- white, unlined paper, a few sheets
- pen
- scissors
- glue stick

✎ old magazines you have permission to cut

✎ colored markers

✎ large poster board, any dimensions

 Safety Precautions

Please review and follow the safety guidelines at the beginning of this volume.

What You Do

1. Answer the questions in the data table as directed, and fill in the blanks honestly. Take your time.

2. Write down your responses on white paper.

3. Read your responses carefully.

4. Look through magazines and find pictures that relate to your responses and represent your likes, dislikes, strengths, and weaknesses. If you cannot find pictures, draw your own on white paper with markers.

5. Cut out the pictures that you have found or drawn.

6. Glue the pictures to your poster board and arrange them in a way so that you feel the pictures represent you. If you are showing something you dislike, think of a way to convey that you do not like the item (for example, Figure 1).

Prohibited sign

Figure 1

Data Table
Relationships Inventory: yes or no
1. I have at least one good friend.
2. I prefer having many friends.
3. I prefer having only a few close friends.
4. I am liked by most people I know.
5. I know an adult I can trust when I need help.
6. I like people who like the same things I do.
7. I like people who like different things than I do.
8. I tend to be a leader.
9. I tend to be follower.
School Inventory (fill in the blanks, or yes or no)
10. My favorite subject is _____.
11. My least favorite subject is _____.
12. I am good at this subject: _____.
13. I am not good at this subject: _____.
14. I like school: _____.
Activities and Interests
15. I am good at _____.

(continued)

16. I want to learn how to _____.

17. I am not good at _____.

18. I like sports: _____.

19. I prefer doing activities by myself: _____.

20. I prefer being involved in group activities: _____.

21. I like being on a team: _____.

22. My hobby is _____.

Stress Relief

23. I relax by _____.

24. When I am stressed, I prefer to be with people: _____.

25. When I am stressed, I prefer to be alone: _____.

26. I have a long-term goal: _____.

Health

27. I eat a balanced diet: _____.

28. I exercise regularly: _____.

29. I like to eat this food: _____.

30. I do not like eating this food: _____.

 **Observations**

1. Did you learn anything new about yourself?

2. If someone were to see your poster, would they learn a lot about you? What would they see?

3. If you have a goal, what steps do you think you would have to do to achieve that goal? If you do not have a long-term goal, based on your board, what might be a good goal for you?

4. No one else's board will look like yours. Why?

Our Findings

Please refer to the Our Findings appendix at the back of this volume.

Further Reading

Kaufman, Gershen, Raphael Lev, and Pamela Espeland. *Stick Up for Yourself: Every Kid's Guide to Personal Power and Positive Self-Esteem.* Minneapolis: Free Spirit Publishing, 1999. Children's book that helps youngsters identify their feelings and understand that they are responsible for their own behavior.

Palmer, Pat, and Melissa Alberti Froehner. *Teen Esteem: A Self-Direction Manual for Young Adults.* Atascadero, CA: Impact Books, 2010. A guide for young adults that helps with refusal skills and maintaining a positive attitude.

"Self-Concept." *International Encyclopedia of the Social Sciences.* 2008. Available online. URL: http://www.encyclopedia.com/doc/1G2-3045302375.html. Accessed December 1, 2010. Discusses the development of self-concept and its impact on self-esteem.

"Self-Esteem." *International Encyclopedia of the Social Sciences*. 2008. Available online. URL: http://www.encyclopedia.com/doc/1G2-3045302385.html. Accessed December 1, 2010. Detailed entry defining self-esteem and how it is impacted.

"The Story of Self-Esteem." *KidsHealth*. 2010. Available Online. URL: http://kidshealth.org/kid/feeling/emotion/self_esteem.html. Accessed December 1, 2010. In story form and in language for children, this Web site provides information about self-esteem.

4. TAKING BLOOD PRESSURE

Introduction

Blood pressure is the result of blood *circulating* through your body and pressing against the walls of the *blood vessels* through which it flows. The force pushing your blood through the blood vessels comes from the pumping of the left *ventricle* of your heart. When health care professionals take your blood pressure, they measure *systole*, the active pumping of blood from your heart's ventricles, and *diastole*, the resting of your heart. Your blood pressure is measured with a device called a *sphygmomanometer*, or blood pressure cuff. The cuff is wrapped around your upper arm and puts pressure on it, closing off the main artery, known as the *brachial artery*, situated in your arm. The person taking your blood pressure places a *stethoscope* just under the cuff and listens to when this artery opens and closes as the air is released from the cuff.

In this activity, you will learn about blood pressure and how to use an appropriate instrument to measure blood pressure.

Time Needed

45 minutes

What You Need

- blood pressure cuff, child size and adult size (can be purchased at any medical supply store or online)
- stethoscope (can be purchased at any medical supply store)
- a friend

✎ an adult

✎ paper, 1 sheet

✎ pen or pencil

✎ computer with Internet access

 Safety Precautions

Please review and follow the safety guidelines at the beginning of this volume. Always follow Internet safety guidelines. Adult supervision is recommended for Internet access and use of blood pressure apparatus.

What You Do

1. Find an adult volunteer who will allow you to take his or her blood pressure.

2. Deflate the bladder of the blood pressure cuff by turning the air valve (Figure 1).

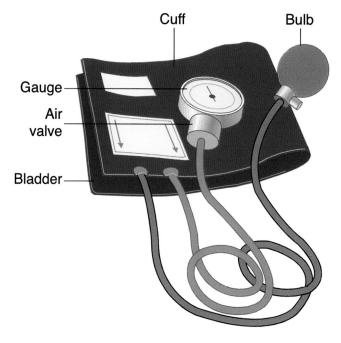

Figure 1

3. Place the cuff around the volunteer's upper arm so that it fits snugly but is not too tight (Figure 2).

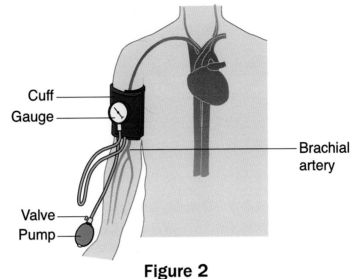

Figure 2

4. Put the ear pieces of the stethoscope in your ears.

5. Place the head of the stethoscope between the cuff and the volunteer's arm (Figure 3).

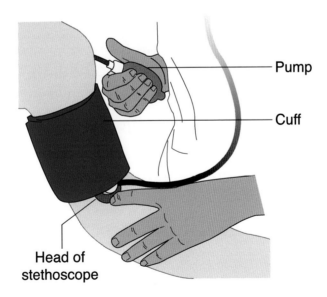

Figure 3

6. Squeeze the bulb to inflate the cuff, while keeping an eye on the pressure gauge. This will take a few squeezes. You will probably not have to go above 150 millimeters (mm) on the gauge (Figure 4).

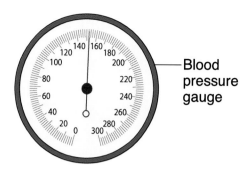

Figure 4

7. Turn the air valve just a little to let the air out slowly enough so that you can watch the gauge and listen through the stethoscope while not letting air out so slowly that your volunteer is uncomfortable.

8. Pay careful attention to the sounds you hear as the pressure falls.

9. When you hear a noise that sounds like "brrrpsh" or "plrrrp," note the pressure on the gauge. This is the systolic blood pressure (the active pumping of blood from the heart).

10. The sound will become louder as more air is released. Note the pressure on the gauge when you stop hearing the sound. This is the diastolic blood pressure, the heart at rest.

11. Release the rest of the air from the cuff.

12. Record your readings on the data table. Blood pressure is written as systolic blood pressure over diastolic blood pressure (e.g., 120/80).

13. Repeat steps 6 to 12 with a volunteer friend.

14. Repeat steps 1 to 13 with a child volunteer, under adult supervision, with the child's cuff.

15. Repeat steps 1 to 13 on yourself.

Data Table				
Blood pressure	**Adult**	**Friend**	**Child**	**Self**
1				
2				
3				
Average reading: (1st + 2nd + 3rd) ÷ 3				

 **Observations**

1. Was it difficult to determine the blood pressure of your volunteers and yourself? Why or why not?

2. Research blood pressure on the Internet. What would be considered high blood pressure? Normal blood pressure?

3. Why do you think it is helpful to track a person's blood pressure over time?

Our Findings

Please refer to the Our Findings appendix at the back of this volume.

Further Reading

"Blood Pressure." The American Heart Association. 2010. Available online. URL: http://www.americanheart.org/presenter. jhtml?identifier=4473. Accessed December 1, 2010. The article explains what the numbers on a blood pressure gauge measure as well as the signs of high blood pressure.

"Blood Pressure." *The Columbia Encyclopedia,* 6th ed. 2008. Available online. URL: http://www.encyclopedia.com/doc/1E1-bloodpre.html. Accessed December 1, 2010. Explains blood pressure, as well as factors that affect blood pressure.

Casey, Aggie, and Herbert Benson. *Harvard Medical School Guide to Lowering Your Blood Pressure.* New York: McGraw-Hill, 2005. Contains easy nutrition and diet guidelines to lower high blood pressure, as well as stress reduction strategies.

"High Blood Pressure." National Heart Lung and Blood Institute. (2008). Available online. URL: http://www.nhlbi.nih.gov/health/dci/Diseases/Hbp/HBP_WhatIs.html. Accessed December 1, 2010. Succinct explanation of what high blood pressure is and the ill effects it causes.

"High Blood Pressure (Hypertension)." The Mayo Clinic. 2008. Available online. URL: http://www.mayoclinic.com/health/high-blood-pressure/DS00100. Accessed December 1, 2010. Defines hypertension and describes the symptoms of high blood pressure.

5. TAKING A PULSE AT MULTIPLE SITES

Introduction

The *ventricles* of the heart squeeze blood through the blood vessels. Each time your heart beats, a *pulse* can be felt in your major *arteries*. One of the easiest places to find on your body for feeling your pulse is on the inside of your wrists; that is where your *radial artery* lies. The radial artery is responsible for delivering blood to your hand. Another common area of the body for checking pulse is on your neck, at the *carotid artery*. The carotid arteries are located on both sides of your neck and deliver *oxygenated* blood to your brain. Though these are common pulse sites, there are several other parts of the body where your pulse can be detected. Pulse sites are important to know in an emergency situation when a health care professional may not be able to touch some parts of a person's body due to injuries. Your pulse can be detected at your *femoral artery*, between your hip and *groin*; at your *brachial artery*, on the upper part of your arm below the *bicep*; at your *popliteal artery*, which is behind your knee; and at your *abdominal aorta*, which is above your belly button, before this major artery splits to lead down to your legs.

In this activity, you will take your pulse rates at each of these sites and determine which parts of the body are the easiest places for detecting a pulse.

Time Needed
40 minutes

What You Need

✎ pen or pencil

✎ stopwatch or watch with seconds hand

Safety Precautions

Please review and follow the safety guidelines at the beginning of this volume.

What You Do

1. Take your radial pulse. To do this, place your second and third fingers on the groove of the inside of your wrist leading down from your thumb (Figure 1).

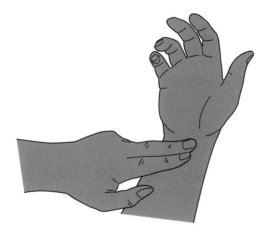

Figure 1. Taking a radial pulse.

2. Rest your fingers lightly on your wrist until you feel your pulse.

3. Count your pulse over the course of 1 minute.

4. Record your pulse on the data table, and note if you had difficulty locating a pulse and if it felt strong or weak to you.

5. Take your carotid pulse. To do this, place your second and third fingers along the outer edge of your trachea (Figure 2). Be careful to take your carotid pulse on one side of your neck at a time so as not to constrict your blood flow to your brain.

Figure 2. Taking a carotid pulse.

6. Repeat steps 3 and 4.

7. Take your femoral pulse. To do this, place your second and third fingers about two-thirds of the way from your hip to your groin area (Figure 3).

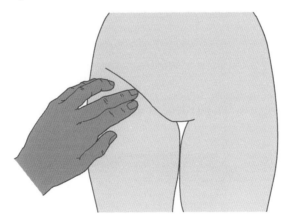

Figure 3. Taking a femoral pulse.

8. Repeat steps 3 and 4.

9. Repeat steps 1 to 4 for each of the following pulses if you are able to feel them: brachial artery, which can be felt when you flex your bicep and place your fingers in the groove between the bicep and the rest of the arm (Figure 4); popliteal artery, which can be felt behind your knee when your knee is slightly bent (Figure 5); and the abdominal aorta, which can be felt above your belly button when you are lying down (Figure 6).

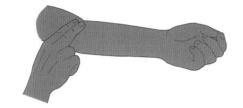

Figure 4. Taking a brachial pulse.

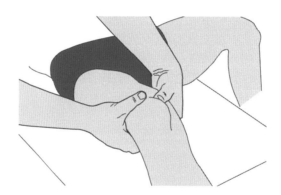

Figure 5. Taking a popliteal pulse.

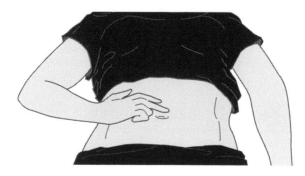

Figure 6. Taking an abdominal pulse.

Data Table			
Pulse	**Pulse rate**	**Easy or difficult to locate?**	**Weak or strong?**
Radial artery			
Carotid artery			
Femoral artery			
Brachial artery			
Popliteal artery			
Abdominal aorta			

 Observations

1. Which pulse was easiest to detect?
2. Which pulse was the most difficult to detect?
3. When might it be helpful to take a pulse in an area different from the wrist?
4. What is the relationship between your pulse and your heart beat?

Our Findings

Please refer to the Our Findings appendix at the back of this volume.

Further Reading

"Artery." *The Columbia Encyclopedia,* 6th ed. 2008. Available online. URL: http://www.encyclopedia.com/doc/1E1-artery.html. Accessed December 1, 2010. A brief entry explaining what an artery is and the kind of tissues that compose an artery.

Bjorklund, Ruth. *Circulatory System: The Amazing Human Body*. Tarrytown, NY: Marshall Cavendish Children's Books, 2008. Illustrated children's book detailing the parts of the circulatory system and how blood is pumped throughout the body.

"Circulatory System." *The Columbia Encyclopedia,* 6th ed. 2008. Available online. URL: http://www.encyclopedia.com/doc/1E1-circulat.html. Accessed December 1, 2010. Detailed entry about the parts of the circulatory system and circulatory disorders.

"Pulse." *The Columbia Encyclopedia,* 6th ed. 2008. Available online. URL: http://www.encyclopedia.com/doc/1E1-pulse1.html. Accessed December 1, 2010. An article explaining what a pulse and a normal pulse rate are.

"Target Heart Rates." American Heart Association. 2010. Available online. URL: http://www.americanheart.org/presenter.jhtml?identifier=4736. Accessed December 1, 2010. Includes a chart indicating target heart rates depending on age.

6. STUDYING NERVES—SENSITIVITY TESTING

Introduction

Our *nervous system* consists of our *central nervous system* and our *peripheral nervous system*. The central nervous system is made up of the brain and the *spinal cord*; the peripheral nervous system is comprised of *neurons*, *ganglia*, and *nerves*. *Sensory* neurons in our nerves receive information from sensory *receptors*. Our nerves allow us to sense pressure, heat, and pain. Different parts of your skin contain more or fewer sensory receptors depending on the need for that part of your body to be able to sense *stimulation*. When our nerves are damaged, we lose the ability to sense heat or pressure, and the risk of further injury is heightened because then an individual will not feel pain or know when to pull away from the source of the pain.

In this activity, you will test a friend's nerve sensitivity on his or her arm and hand, then use that information to map areas of low and high concentrations of receptors.

Time Needed

40 minutes

What You Need

✎ 5 index cards

✎ 9 paper clips

✎ transparent tape, at least 9 pieces

✎ ruler

✎ 1 sheet white paper, at least as big as your arm

✎ pen or pencil

✎ a friend

✎ markers or crayons, 5 different colors

Safety Precautions

Please review and follow the safety guidelines at the beginning of this volume.

What You Do

1. Partially unbend all 9 paper clips (Figure 1).

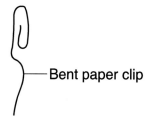

—Bent paper clip

Figure 1

2. Tape 1 paper clip to the bottom center of an index card so that the unbent part of the clip sticks down past the card (Figure 2).

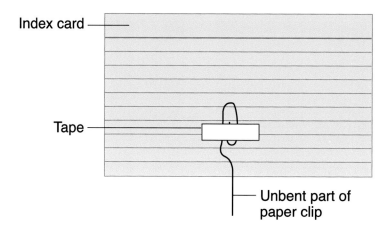

Index card

Tape

Unbent part of paper clip

Figure 2

3. Tape 2 paper clips 0.2 in. (0.5 cm) apart on an index card (Figure 3).

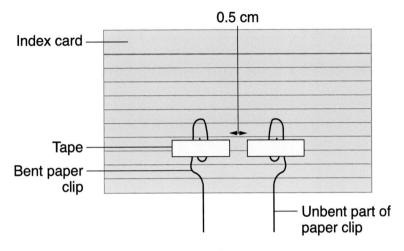

Figure 3

4. Repeat step 3 with the next 3 index cards, except space the paper clips 0.4 in. (1 cm) apart, 0.8 in. (2 cm) apart, and 1.2 in. (3 cm) apart, respectively.

5. Ask your friend to close his or her eyes.

6. Mix up the cards so that they are in no particular order.

7. Touch your friend's upper arm with the paper clip's unbent end of one of the cards (Figure 4).

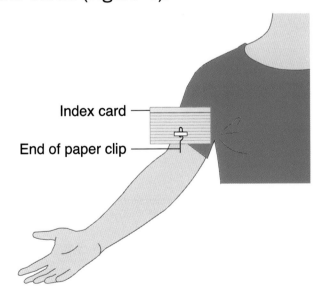

Figure 4

8. Ask your friend if you touched his or her arm with one paper clip or two.

9. Record on the data table if your friend was correct or incorrect.

10. Repeat steps 5 to 9 with the rest of the cards.

11. Repeat steps 5 to 9 on your friend's forearm, palm, and fingertips.

12. Trace your friend's arm onto the white paper (Figure 5).

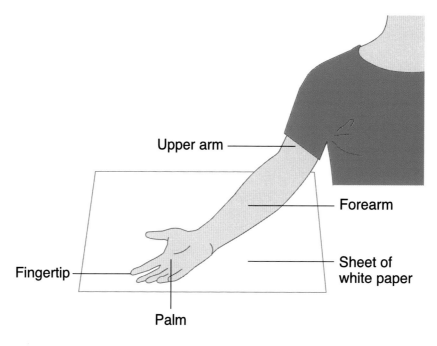

Figure 5

13. Using the information from your data table and the color key in Data Table 1, make a map of your friend's skin sensitivity by coloring in the picture you drew of your friend's arm with the appropriate colors.

Data Table 1		
Part of arm	**Number correct responses**	**Number incorrect responses**
Upper arm		
Forearm		
Palm		
Fingertips		

Data Table 2	
Number correct responses	**Color**
1	blue
2	green
3	yellow
4	orange
5	red

 Observations

1. Which parts were the most sensitive? How could you tell?
2. Which parts were the least sensitive? How could you tell?
3. Why do you need more nerve receptors in some parts of your hand and not in others?
4. How would nerve sensitivity mapping be useful for someone with an injury?

Our Findings

Please refer to the Our Findings appendix at the back of this volume.

Further Reading

"Brain." *The Columbia Encyclopedia,* 6th ed. 2008. Available online. URL: http://www.encyclopedia.com/doc/1E1-brain.html. Accessed December 1, 2010. Discusses the parts of the brain, neural pathways, and brain research.

"Neurologic Diseases." 2009. National Library of Medicine. Available online. URL: http://www.nlm.nih.gov/medlineplus/ neurologicdiseases.html. Accessed December 1, 2010. Provides links to many types of diseases that can affect the nervous system.

"Neurology." *The Columbia Encyclopedia,* 6th ed. 2008. Available online. URL: http://www.encyclopedia.com/doc/1E1-neurolog.html. Accessed December 1, 2010. Definition of neurology, and a study of the human nervous system and its disorders.

Stein Carter, J. 2004. "Nervous System and Senses." Available online. URL: http://biology.clc.uc.edu/courses/Bio105/nervous.htm. Accessed December 1, 2010. Concise definitions of the parts of the nervous system and their relation to our five senses.

"Synapse." *The Columbia Encyclopedia,* 6th ed. 2008. Available online. URL: http://www.encyclopedia.com/doc/1E1-synapse.html. Accessed December 1, 2010. Explains how nerve impulses travel from neuron to neuron.

7. SIMULATING THE NEGATIVE EFFECTS OF TOBACCO—PART 1

Introduction

Many young people take up smoking, evidently ignorant of the fact that smoking can cause lung disease, heart disease, *stroke*, and *cancer*. Unfortunately, these long-term effects do not dissuade some people from smoking because they feel like they will not experience these illnesses until later in life, if ever. However, there are also many consequences from smoking. *Tobacco* contains more than 40 chemicals, including a poison called *nicotine*. Nicotine is known to increase heart rate, *constrict blood vessels*, and raise *blood pressure*, all of which put an enormous *strain* on the heart. These effects can occur to the body in less than 4 seconds. However, nicotine is not the only dangerous substance found in tobacco. Cigarettes also produce *carbon monoxide*, the same poisonous gas found in car *exhaust*. Smoking cigarettes delivers carbon monoxide to the *bloodstream*, reducing the oxygen levels in the blood.

In this experiment, you will simulate the effects of nicotine on the heart and blood vessels, as well as the *absorption* of carbon monoxide into the bloodstream.

Time Needed

30 minutes

What You Need

- bicycle pump
- 2 small, plastic cups

- ✎ drinking straw
- ✎ coffee stirrer
- ✎ small, empty water bottle
- ✎ coffee grounds, about 1/2 teaspoon (2.5 grams)
- ✎ blue food coloring, a few drops
- ✎ water, enough to fill both cups and the water bottle
- ✎ stopwatch or watch with seconds hand
- ✎ a friend
- ✎ paper, lined or unlined, 1 sheet
- ✎ pen or pencil

Safety Precautions

Please review and follow the safety guidelines at the beginning of this volume.

What You Do

1. Pump the bicycle pump several times.
2. Note how much or little pressure it takes to force air out of the pump.
3. Ask a friend to obstruct the flow of air by stepping on the hose leading out of the pump (Figure 1).

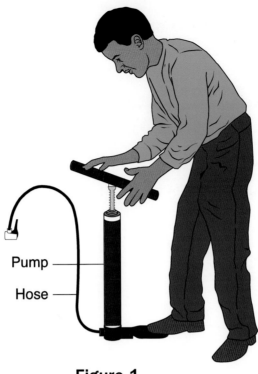

Figure 1

4. Pump the bicycle pump several times.

5. Note any difference in the effort and pressure you must now use to try to force air out of the pump, and record your observations on the data table.

Data Table	
Observations about pumping	Observations about pumping with air flow obstructed
Time with straw	Time with coffee stirrer

(continued)

Time for coffee grounds to change color of water	Time for food coloring to change color of water

6. Fill the 2 small, plastic cups about halfway with equal amounts of water.

7. Insert the drinking straw into one cup and the coffee stirrer into the other (Figure 2).

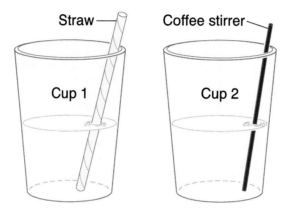

Figure 2

8. Have your friend time how long it takes you to drink all the water from the first cup through the straw.

9. Record the time, and record your observations on the data table.

10. Have your friend time how long it takes you to drink all the water from the second cup through the coffee stirrer.

11. Record the time, and record your observations on the data table.

12. Fill the small water bottle about 2/3 full with water.

13. Add 1/2 teaspoon (2.5 grams) of coffee grounds to the water in the bottle.

14. Note how quickly or slowly the coffee grounds color the water, and record your observations on the data table.

15. Add 1 drop of blue food coloring to the same bottle.

16. Note how quickly or slowly it colors the water, and record your observations on the data table.

 Observations

1. What part of your body does the pump represent? If the effects of tobacco are simulated by placing a foot on the hose of the pump, what can you deduce about the effects of tobacco on that organ of your body?

2. Tobacco causes blood vessels to constrict. How do the straws and water model this effect?

3. If the coffee grounds represent oxygen, food coloring represents the carbon monoxide in cigarettes, and the water represents your blood, what can you say about the rate at which your body absorbs the poisonous carbon monoxide from cigarettes as opposed to the oxygen you need from the air?

Our Findings

Please refer to the Our Findings appendix at the back of this volume.

Further Reading

"Cigarette Smoking and Cardiovascular Disease." American Heart Association. 2010. Available online. URL: http://www.americanheart. org/presenter.jhtml?identifier=4545. Accessed December 1, 2010. Includes facts about the impact of smoking on the heart, diseases that smoking causes, and the effects of secondhand smoke.

"NIDA Infofacts: Cigarettes and Other Tobacco Products." 2009. Available online. URL: http://www.drugabuse.gov/Infofacts/tobacco. html. Accessed December 1, 2010. The official government Web site of the National Institute on Drug Abuse, detailing the effects of tobacco on various organs of the body and describing treatments to help people quite smoking.

Silverstein, Alvin, Virginia Silverstein, and Laura Silverstein Nunn. *Smoking (My Health)*. Danbury, CT: Children's Press, 2004. Children's book about how smoking harms the body, as well as tips on avoiding the habit.

"Smoking and Tobacco Use." Center for Disease Control. 2009. Available online. URL: http://www.cdc.gov/tobacco/. Accessed December 1, 2010. Official government Web site containing links to latest research reports on the effects of smoking on the body.

Tobacco.org. 2010. Available online. URL: http://www.tobacco.org/. Accessed December 1, 2010. Web site with most up-to-date links for top news stories related to tobacco.

8. SIMULATING THE NEGATIVE EFFECTS OF TOBACCO—PART 2

Introduction

Among the many harmful substances found in tobacco is *tar*. Tar is extremely sticky and, when inhaled, coats the lungs. When tar covers the *air sacs* inside the lungs, the body is unable to *absorb a sufficient* amount of oxygen. Eventually, the tar also damages the *cilia* of the *respiratory system*, which normally function to remove dust, dirt, and *pollen particles* from the air passages. Instead, these particles are not removed from the air passages but stay inside the person's respiratory system. Tar alone contains numerous *carcinogens* that can affect the mouth, throat, *larynx*, lungs, kidneys, and bladder. Some smokers purchase cigarettes that are rated lower in tar than others because they believe lower tar cigarettes will be less harmful than ordinary brands. However, these ratings are produced using a smoking machine and do not reflect the actual amounts of tar an individual may *inhale*. Also, some cigarettes claim to have reduced tar but actually may only provide holes for more air to be inhaled by the smoker. But when the smoker inhales, he or she may unknowingly cover these holes and therefore inhale more tar.

In this activity, you will simulate the effects of tar on the respiratory system.

Time Needed

30 minutes

What You Need

✎ glass jar with lid, 1/2 pint (237 ml) size

✎   molasses, 10 to 12 ounces (oz) (284 to 341 ml)

✎   2 coffee filters

✎   funnel

✎   small paintbrush

✎   beaker

✎   water, enough to fill the beaker twice

✎   a place to pour out the water

✎   measuring cup

 ## Safety Precautions

Please review and follow the safety guidelines at the beginning of this volume.

What You Do

1. Pour about 8 oz (227 ml) of molasses into the jar.
2. Close the lid tightly.
3. Move the jar around to coat the sides with the molasses (Figure 1).

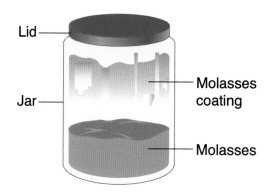

Figure 1

4. Observe the jar. The amount of molasses in the jar is the equivalent to the amount of tar that accumulates in the lungs of

a smoker over a 1-year period if he or she smokes a pack a day. Record your observations on the data table.

Data Table	
Observations about jar of molasses as model for lungs with tar	
Rate of water through filter and observations	
Rate of water through molasses-covered filter and observations	

5. Line the funnel with a coffee filter (Figure 2).

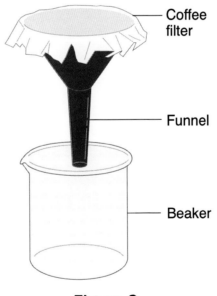

Coffee filter

Funnel

Beaker

Figure 2

6. Insert the funnel into the mouth of the beaker.
7. Pour water through the funnel into the beaker, noting the rate at which the water flows into the beaker, and record your observations on the data table.

8. Remove the wet filter from the funnel and pour out the water.

9. With the paintbrush, coat the other filter with molasses (Figure 3).

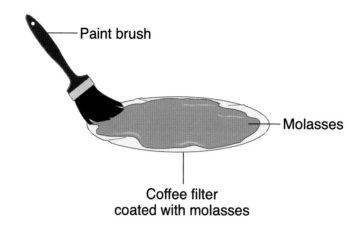

Figure 3

11. Pour water through the funnel into the beaker, noting the rate at which the water flows into the beaker, and record your observations on the data table.

 Observations

1. How did the look of the molasses in the jar make you feel about the buildup of tar in the lungs caused by smoking?

2. Did the water flow faster or slower with the molasses-coated filter inside the funnel as opposed to the plain filter?

3. How did the molasses and filter simulate the effects of tar on the respiratory system?

Our Findings

Please refer to the Our Findings appendix at the back of this volume.

Further Reading

"Cigar and Cigarette." *The Columbia Encyclopedia,* 6th ed. 2008. Available online. URL: http://www.encyclopedia.com/doc/1E1-cigarNci.html. Accessed December 1, 2010. Description of what cigars and cigarettes are, their uses, and their dangers.

Malaspina, Ann. *False Images, Deadly Promises: Smoking and the Media.* Broomall, PA: Mason Crest Publishers, 2008. A book for young adults that exposes how the tobacco industry tries to recruit teens and children to smoke, even though the industry is banned from direct advertising to that audience.

"Stop Smoking." American Lung Association. 2010. Available online. URL: http://www.lungusa.org/stop-smoking/. Accessed December 1, 2010. Tips and links from the American Lung Association on how to quit smoking.

"Tobacco." *The Columbia Encyclopedia,* 6th ed. 2008. Available online. URL: http://www.encyclopedia.com/doc/1E1-tobacco.html. Accessed December 1, 2010. Encyclopedia entry that explains the history and uses of tobacco.

"Up in Smoke: The Truth About Tar and Nicotine Ratings." Federal Trade Commission. 2000. Available online. URL: http://www.ftc.gov/bcp/edu/pubs/consumer/alerts/alt069.shtm. Accessed December 1, 2010. Government Web site that explains the truth behind tar ratings of cigarettes.

9. TOOTH CARE—PART 1: FLUORIDE

Introduction

The foods you eat contain *substances* that your body needs. When some of these foods are allowed to remain on the surfaces of your teeth, food particles can lead to *dental caries*, or *cavities*. The *bacteria* commonly found in your mouth along with your *saliva* change the sugars in your food to a sticky substance known as *dental plaque*. Bacteria *thrive* on plaque and, as a result, multiply and produce *acids* that eat away at *tooth enamel*. When the *calcium* of the tooth enamel is worn away, a hole forms in the tooth enamel, resulting in a cavity. In addition, plaque can cause bad breath and gum disease. The best ways to reduce or eliminate the buildup of plaque is to brush and floss daily, as well as see a dentist every 6 months. Brushing properly with a *fluoride* toothpaste is essential to healthy teeth and cavity prevention. Fluoride attracts *minerals* to the tooth's surface and enhances the tooth's ability to *remineralize*.

In this experiment, you will compare the effect of an acid on a surface when it is and is not protected by fluoride.

Time Needed

40 minutes to set up, 5 days to complete

What You Need

- egg
- black marker
- clear nail polish

- ✎   2 Pyrex® measuring cups
- ✎   vinegar, enough to cover the egg (see item 10)
- ✎   paper towel
- ✎   faucet with flowing water
- ✎   plastic wrap
- ✎   teaspoon
- ✎   1 tube of toothpaste containing fluoride

Safety Precautions

Please review and follow the safety guidelines at the beginning of this volume.

What You Do

1. Allow the egg to warm to room temperature.
2. Draw an X on one side of the egg (Figure 1).

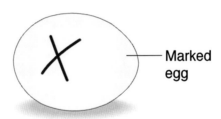

Marked egg

Figure 1

3. Paint over the X with clear nail polish. This will prevent it from being eaten away by the vinegar, to be applied in item 10.
4. Squeeze all of the toothpaste out of the tube into the measuring cup.
5. Using the teaspoon, push down on the toothpaste in the cup to remove air bubbles and level the toothpaste (Figure 2).

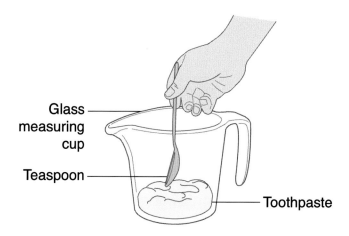

Figure 2

6. When you are sure the nail polish (in item 3) has dried, carefully nestle the egg with the X facing down into the toothpaste in the cup so that the egg is half buried (Figure 3).

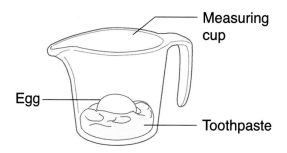

Figure 3

7. Cover the cup with plastic wrap and set aside for 4 days.

8. Remove the egg from the toothpaste and rinse it with lukewarm water.

9. Once the egg has dried completely—give it several hours to dry—gently place the egg into the clean measuring cup.

10. Cover the egg with vinegar. Use the teaspoon to hold the egg down under the vinegar.

11. Set the teaspoon on top of the egg, with the handle leaning on the side of the measuring cup (Figure 4).

Figure 4

12. Cover the cup with plastic wrap, with the teaspoon in place.

13. Observe the side of the egg not marked with the X.

14. Set aside the egg in the vinegar for about 8 or 9 hours.

15. Remove the egg from the vinegar.

16. Carefully wash the egg with lukewarm water.

17. Gently touch or tap the side of the egg marked with the X.

18. Gently touch or tap the side of the egg that was not marked with the X.

 **Observations**

1. When you first placed the egg into the vinegar, what did you observe about the side of the egg not marked with an X and therefore not treated with the fluoride in the toothpaste?

2. After removing the egg from the vinegar and touching each side, what difference did you notice between the two sides?

3. What do you think protected one-half of the egg?

4. How does this simulate protecting your teeth from cavities?

Our Findings

Please refer to the Our Findings appendix at the back of this volume.

Further Reading

ADA.org 2010. Available online. URL: http://www.ada.org/. Accessed December 1, 2010. Official Web site of the American Dental Association, containing articles, information, and links about tooth and gum care.

ADHA.org. 2010. American Dental Hygienists' Association. Available online. URL: http://www.adha.org/. Accessed December 1, 2010. This official Web site of the American Dental Hygienists' Association provides links and information on oral health.

Lee, Benjamin. *Things You Should Know About Teeth: Dental Health Guide*. Buckinghamshire, UK: AuthorHouse, 2007. Detailed tips from a longtime dentist regarding preventing dental issues and explaining dental procedures.

"Oral Health Resources." 2010. Center for Disease Control. Available online. URL: http://www.cdc.gov/OralHealth/. Accessed December 1, 2010. Information from the CDC on preventing cavities, gum disease, and infections of the mouth.

"Teeth." *The Columbia Encyclopedia,* 6th ed. 2008. Available online. URL: http://www.encyclopedia.com/doc/1E1-teeth.html. Accessed December 1, 2010. Entry about teeth, tooth care, and the positive effects of fluoridation.

10. TOOTH CARE—PART 2: TOOTH DECAY

Introduction

Most of us have learned to brush our teeth with toothpaste on a daily basis and to see the dentist regularly. However, this is not doing enough to prevent *cavities* and *gum disease*. Small *particles* of food get trapped between your teeth where your toothbrush cannot reach. This situation may lead to cavities forming on the inner sides of both teeth, on each side of where the food is trapped. Some food also gets trapped under your gums. To remove food particles before they lead to *dental plaque accumulation*, you must *floss* daily. Flossing allows you to scrape food out from between your teeth and, when done properly, also removes food stuck at or just below the gumline. Failure to do so leads to cavities, tooth loss, bad breath, and serious gum disease.

In this experiment, you will first simulate the necessity of flossing versus just brushing, and then test foods for the presence of sugars that can lead to plaque buildup between teeth.

Time Needed
60 to 90 minutes

What You Need

- latex glove (use a non-latex glove if you or your friend have a latex allergy)
- peanut butter (enough to attend to item 3)
- plastic or rubber spatula

- toothbrush
- toothpaste
- floss, about 18 inches (in.) (46 centimeters [cm])
- a friend
- Benedict's solution, about 5 ounces (oz) (150 milliliters [ml])
- 5 test tubes
- test-tube rack
- tongs
- alcohol burner
- small piece each of 5 different foods (e.g., cracker, bread, cookie, etc.)

Safety Precautions

Please review and follow the safety guidelines at the beginning of this volume. Adult supervision is required when using an open flame and heating substances. Wear goggles and point a test tube away from yourself and others while heating the test tube.

What You Do

1. Have your friend place the latex glove on one hand.
2. Ask your friend to spread her or his fingers open (Figure 1).

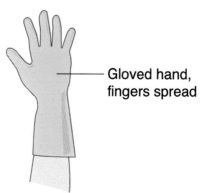

Gloved hand, fingers spread

Figure 1

3. Using the spatula, spread peanut butter between all the fingers.

4. Have your friend put her or his fingers together (Figure 2).

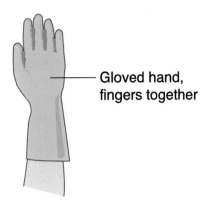

Gloved hand,
fingers together

Figure 2

5. Squeeze some toothpaste on a toothbrush.

6. Try to scrub the peanut butter out from between your friend's fingers without her opening her fingers.

7. Observe the results.

8. Now try using dental floss to remove the peanut butter by gripping the floss between the fingers of both hands and working your way down in between your friend's fingers, scraping the length of each finger (Figure 3).

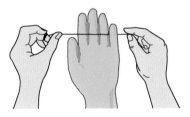

Figure 3

9. Clean up the materials you used.

10. Place a small piece of food in a test tube.

11. Record the name of the food on the data table.

12. Add 30 ml (1 oz) of Benedict's solution to the test tube.

13. Using the tongs to hold the test tube, heat the test tube over the alcohol burner (Figure 4).

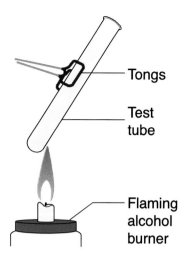

Figure 4

14. Observe any color change. Benedict's solution is blue; the presence of sugar in a substance will turn the solution orange.

15. Record the results on the data table.

16. Repeat steps 10 to 15 four more times, using a clean test tube and a different food each time.

Data Table			
Test tube	**Name of food**	**Color change to orange?**	**Contains sugar?**
1			
2			
3			
4			
5			

 **Observations**

1. Which method was more successful at removing the food between the fingers, brushing or floss?

2. How does the successful effort simulate flossing your teeth?

3. What do you think will happen to your teeth if you do not floss?

4. When you heated the food treated with Benedict's solution, which foods contained sugar? Were you surprised by any of the results?

5. What do you think is the consequence of allowing sugars to remain between your teeth if you fail to floss and only brush your teeth?

Our Findings

Please refer to the Our Findings appendix at the back of this volume.

Further Reading

ADA.org 2010. Available online. URL: http://www.ada.org/. Accessed December 1, 2010. Official Web site of the American Dental Association, containing articles, information, and links about tooth and gum care.

ADHA.org. 2010. American Dental Hygienists' Association. Available online. URL: http://www.adha.org/. Accessed December 1, 2010. The official Web site of the American Dental Hygienists' Association provides links and information on oral health.

"How to Floss—Flossing Tips." Colgate. 2010. Available online. URL: http://www.colgate.com/app/Colgate/US/OC/Information/ OralHealthBasics/GoodOralHygiene/BrushingandFlossing/ HowtoFloss.cvsp. Accessed December 1, 2010. Tips on how to floss properly from one of the leading brands of dental hygiene products.

Lee, Benjamin. *Things You Should Know About Teeth: Dental Health Guide*. Buckinghamshire, UK: AuthorHouse, 2007. Detailed tips from a longtime dentist regarding the prevention of dental issues and an explanation of dental procedures.

"Oral Health Resources." 2010. Center for Disease Control. Available online. URL: http://www.cdc.gov/OralHealth/. Accessed December 1, 2010. Information from the CDC on preventing cavities, gum disease, and infections of the mouth.

11. MODELING BLOOD ALCOHOL CONTENT

Introduction

In the United States, it is illegal for anyone under the age of 21 to purchase or *consume* alcohol. Underage people may not understand the risks involved with drinking alcohol. Alcohol *impairs* a person's ability to drive, slows reaction times, causes balance problems, and creates other health issues. People who drink and drive, no matter what their age, run the risk of causing serious injury or death to themselves and others. If a police officer pulls a car over at a traffic stop and *suspects* that the driver may have been drinking, the officer will attempt to *ascertain* the person's *Blood Alcohol Content*, or BAC. It is illegal to drive with a BAC over the limit set by that state.

In this activity, you will simulate some of the effects of alcohol on the body and learn to calculate BAC.

Time Needed

45 minutes

What You Need

- 2 friends
- beanbag
- pen or pencil
- computer with Internet access

Safety Precautions

Please review and follow the safety guidelines at the beginning of this volume. Always follow Internet safety guidelines. Adult supervision is recommended for Internet access.

What You Do

1. Have your friends stand about 10 to 15 feet (3 to 4.6 meters [m]) apart from each other.

2. Hand one of them a beanbag, and ask your friends to toss it back and forth 10 times to each other, trying not to drop it (Figure 1).

Beanbag

Figure 1

3. Record on Data Table 1 how many times the beanbag was dropped.

4. Spin your friends around several times until they feel somewhat dizzy (Figure 2).

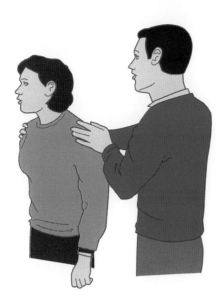

Figure 2

5. Repeat steps 1 to 3.

6. Allow your friends to rest and regain their balance.

7. Ask them to repeat steps 1 to 3 while holding their dominant hand over one eye (Figure 3).

Figure 3

8. Using the computer, research the legal BAC level in your state.

9. Calculate what your BAC level would be for 6 alcoholic drinks using the Web site URL: http://www.ou.edu/oupd/bac.htm or http://www.bloodalcoholcalculator.org/ and Data Table 2.

Data Table 1	
Condition of participating friends	**Number of times beanbag was dropped out of 10 throws**
No impairment	
Dizzy	
Visually impaired	

Data Table 2	
Number of alcoholic drinks	**Your theoretical BAC**
1	
2	
3	
4	
5	
6	

 Observations

1. What difference did you notice in the number of times that your friends dropped the beanbags when they were impaired versus not impaired?

2. How do you think this relates to drinking and driving?

3. What is the legal BAC of a driver under 21 in your state? What is the legal BAC of a driver over 21 in your state?

4. Based on Data Table 2, how many drinks would it take to put someone of your weight over the legal BAC for driving?

Our Findings

Please refer to the Our Findings appendix at the back of this volume.

Further Reading

Bjorklund, Dennis. *Drunk Driving Laws: Rules of the Road When Crossing State Lines, 2nd edition*. Coralville, IA: Praetorian Publishing, 2008. Comprehensive guide to legal BAC limits in the 50 United States, as well as possible legal consequences in each state for driving under the influence.

MADD.org. 2010. *Mothers Against Drunk Driving*. Available online. URL: http://www.madd.org/. Accessed December 1, 2010. Official Web site of an organization dedicated to keeping drunk drivers off the road and educating people about the risks of drunk driving.

Romach, Myroslava, Karen Parker, and Frederick Grittner. "Breathalyzer." *Encyclopedia of Drugs, Alcohol, and Addictive Behavior*. 2001. Available online. URL: http://www.encyclopedia.com/doc/1G2-3403100090.html. Accessed December 1, 2010. Regarding a device for calculating BAC by analyzing a person's breath.

———."Driving Under the Influence (DUI)." *Encyclopedia of Drugs, Alcohol, and Addictive Behavior*. 2001. Available online. URL: http://www.encyclopedia.com/doc/1G2-3403100170.html. Accessed December 1, 2010. Explains what a DUI is and the correlation between BAC and fatal crashes.

"The Police Notebook." Oklahoma University Police Department. 2009. Available online. URL: http://www.ou.edu/oupd/bac.htm. Accessed December 1, 2010. Includes charts on blood alcohol content for both males and females, tips on preventing drunk driving, and an online BAC calculator.

12. EVALUATING STRESSORS

Introduction

Stress is a mental or emotional *strain.* Unfortunately, there are many sources of stress in our lives. We can be affected by high levels of stress from our *environments*, such as our work environment, school environment, or a polluted environment. We can also stress ourselves through poor health, low *self-esteem*, and lack of *coping* skills. We have control over some of our *stressors*, but definitely not over all of them. One of the highest stressors a person can experience is the death of a close family member. We cannot control death, but there are some stressors that we can eliminate from or reduce in our lives, while there are others with which we must learn to deal. Having a plan to reduce stress is important because high levels of stress can lead to serious illness. Stress affects our *hormone* levels, can impact *digestion*, sleeping patterns, heart rates, *blood pressure*, and the *immune system*.

In this activity, you will evaluate your stress levels and work on a plan to reduce your stress levels.

Time Needed

40 minutes

What You Need

- ✎ Social Readjustment Rating Scale (provided as Data Table 1), created by social scientists Thomas Holmes and Richard Rahe
- ✎ pen or pencil
- ✎ paper, a few sheets, lined or unlined

Safety Precautions

Please review and follow the safety guidelines at the beginning of this volume.

What You Do

1. On Data Table 1, mark off each life event that has occurred to you or to someone in your family over the past 12 months. If the same event has occurred more than once during the last 12 months, multiply the number of points associated with that event by the number of occurrences.

2. Add up your "stress" points.

3. Check your total points against Data Table 2 to determine your stress levels and the likelihood of your susceptibilty to illness.

4. Consider the stressors you marked off, and consider if you have control over changing any of them.

5. Make a plan for reducing those stressors over which you have control.

6. Consider those stressors over which you have no control.

7. Make a list of activities that help you relax. When you are feeling stressed, you can use this list to give you ideas on how to relax and reduce your stress levels.

Data Table 1		
Life event	Value	Total Points
Death of spouse	100	
Divorce	73	

(continued)

Marital separation	65	
Jail term	63	
Death of close family member	63	
Personal injury or illness	53	
Marriage	50	
Fired at work	47	
Marital reconciliation	45	
Retirement	45	
Change in health of family member	44	
Pregnancy	40	
Addition of new family member	39	
Business readjustment	39	
Change in financial state	38	
Death of close friend	37	
Change to a different line of work	36	
Change in number of arguments with spouse	35	
Mortgage more than $40,000	31	
Foreclosure or mortgage or loan	30	
Change in responsibilities at work	29	

(continued)

Son or daughter leaving home	29	
Trouble with in-laws	29	
Outstanding personal achievement	28	
Spouse begins or stops work	26	
Begin or end school	26	
Change in living conditions	25	
Revision of personal habits	24	
Trouble with boss	23	
Change in work hours or conditions	20	
Change in residence	20	
Change in schools	20	
Change in recreation	19	
Change in religious activities	19	
Change in social activities	18	
Mortgage or loan of less than $40,000	17	
Change in number of family get-togethers	15	
Change in sleeping habits	15	
Change in eating habits	15	
TOTAL		

Data Table 2		
Points total	Stress level	Likelihood or susceptibility to illness (percent of total points)
300 or more	overstressed/high stress	high (80%)
150–299	some stress	medium (50%)
Under 150	low stress	low (30%)

 **Observations**

1. What was the total of your "stress" points?
2. Are there any stressors over which you have control?
3. What changes do you think you could make to reduce stressors or learn how to relax?
4. How is stress linked to illness?

Our Findings

Please refer to the Our Findings appendix at the back of this volume.

Further Reading

Frey, Rebecca J. "Stress." *Gale Encyclopedia of Mental Disorders*. 2003. Available online. URL: http://www.encyclopedia.com/doc/1G2-3405700371.html. Accessed December 1, 2010. Detailed entry about the impact of stress on physical health.

"Meditation." *The Columbia Encyclopedia,* 6th ed. 2008. Available online. URL: http://www.encyclopedia.com/doc/1E1-meditatn.html. Accessed December 1, 2010. A short entry about meditation, which is considered an excellent relaxation technique.

"101 Strategies for Coping with Stress." 2003. University of Minnesota. Available online. URL: http://www.uccs.umn.edu/oldsite/lasc/handouts/copingstress.html. Accessed December 1, 2010. A list of ways to reduce stress in your life.

Sapolsky, Robert. *Why Zebras Don't Get Ulcers, 3rd ed*. New York: Holt, 2004. Important information linking stress to disease, told in a humorous manner.

"Social Readjustment Rating Scale." 2003. University of Minnesota. Available online. URL: http://www.uccs.umn.edu/oldsite/lasc/handouts/socialreadjustment.html. Accessed December 1, 2010. Includes a version of Thomas Holmes's and Richard Rahe's Social Readjustment Scale as well as links for dealing with stress.

13. COMPARING VITAMIN-C CONTENT

Introduction

Vitamin C is a *water soluble* vitamin also known as *ascorbic acid.* It is a *nutrient* we require that our bodies cannot make. Vitamin C has many benefits for the human body, including boosting the *immune system*, providing *antioxidants*, keeping gums healthy, healing wounds, and producing *collagen*. Failure to take vitamin C may result in the disease known as *scurvy*. Most *multivitamins* contain adequate amounts of vitamin C, and vitamin-C *supplements* are easy to purchase. The best sources of vitamin C are fruits, especially *citrus* fruits such as oranges and grapefruits. However, vitamin C is also found in many vegetables, such as broccoli and parsley. Drinking orange juice is a quick way to ensure that you take in vitamin C.

In this experiment, you will compare the amounts of vitamin C found in fresh squeezed orange juice to that of orange juice made from *concentrate*.

Time Needed

1 hour

What You Need

- water, about 13.5 ounces (oz) (400 milliliters [ml])
- cornstarch, 1 tablespoon (15 grams [g])
- iodine, 10 to 20 drops
- 3 test tubes, 0.5 oz (15 ml) each
- test-tube rack

- ✎   an orange
- ✎   orange juice made from concentrate, 1/4 cup (59 ml)
- ✎   white paper, 1 sheet
- ✎   beaker
- ✎   4 medicine droppers
- ✎   graduated cylinder
- ✎   pot, to hold more than 9 oz water
- ✎   tablespoon
- ✎   watch, clock, or timer
- ✎   stove top
- ✎   plastic cup

Safety Precautions

Please review and follow the safety guidelines at the beginning of this volume. Adult supervision is recommended when using a stove top. An increase in intake of any vitamin source like orange juice should be discussed with parents and their physician.

What You Do

1.   Add 1 tablespoon of cornstarch to the pot.
2.   Mix in enough water to make a paste.
3.   Add 8.5 oz (250 ml) of water to the pot.
4.   Boil the starch solution for 5 minutes.
5.   Add 2.5 oz (75 ml) of water to the beaker.
6.   Using the dropper, add 10 drops of the starch solution to the water.
7.   Using another dropper, add iodine to the starch and water solution until it is a dark indigo color. This is your indicator solution.

8. Add 0.17 oz (5 ml) of the indicator solution to each of the 3 test tubes (Figure 1).

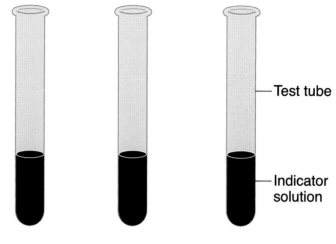

Figure 1

9. Set 1 test tube aside as the control.

10. Squeeze the juice from an orange into the plastic cup.

11. Using a dropper, add 10 drops of the fresh squeezed orange juice to the second test tube (Figure 2).

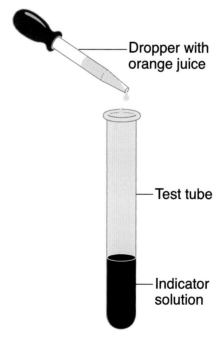

Figure 2

12. Using another dropper, add 10 drops of the orange juice made from concentrate to the third test tube.

13. Line up the test tubes in the test-tube rack.

14. Hold a white sheet of paper behind the test tubes and compare the colors of the solutions. The more vitamin C there is in a sample, the lighter the color of the solution in the test tube. Record your observations on the data table.

Data Table	
Test Tube	**Color and other observations**
Control	
Fresh orange juice	
Orange juice from concentrate	

 Observations

1. Which test tube had the lightest-color solution? What does that tell you about the vitamin-C content of that test tube?

2. Compare the colors of the solution in the test tube with the fresh squeezed orange juice to that made from concentrate. Did they turn the same color? Why or why not?

3. Do you think you are getting the same amount of vitamin C when you drink orange juice made from a concentrate as you would when you drink fresh squeezed orange juice? Explain.

Our Findings

Please refer to the Our Findings appendix at the back of this volume.

Further Reading

"Antioxidant." *The Columbia Encyclopedia,* 6th ed. 2008. Available online. URL: http://www.encyclopedia.com/doc/1E1-antiox.html. Accessed December 1, 2010. Description of how antioxidants help absorb free radicals and keep you healthy.

Bown, Stephen. *Scurvy: How a Surgeon, a Mariner, and a Gentleman Solved the Greatest Medical Mystery of the Age of Sail*. New York: St. Martin's Griffin, 2005. Details the history of scurvy among sailors and how the simple solution of changing their diet cured and prevented the disease.

Pressman, Alan, and Sheila Buff. *The Complete Idiot's Guide to Vitamins and Minerals,* 3rd ed. Exton, PA: Alpha, 2007. Comprehensive coverage of vitamins and minerals, their sources, and why you need them.

"Scurvy." *The Columbia Encyclopedia,* 6th ed. 2008. Available online. URL: http://www.encyclopedia.com/doc/1E1-scurvy.html. Accessed December 1, 2010. Explains the symptoms of scurvy, resulting from lack of vitamin C, and how sailors prevented getting the disease by eating lemons and limes.

"Vitamin." *The Columbia Encyclopedia,* 6th ed. 2008. Available online. URL: http://www.encyclopedia.com/doc/1E1-vitamin.html. Accessed December 1, 2010. Detailed entry about the different vitamins required by the human body, as well as their sources.

14. FOOD PRESERVATION

Introduction

Food preservation is not a modern concept. Back in what we might refer to as "caveman" times, the first type of preservation was the discovery of use of fire to cook meat. Cooking *pasteurizes* the meat, allowing for a longer "shelf-life."

In ancient Egypt, food was preserved with salt or by drying. Europeans later realized that cheese and sausage could be preserved by keeping their moisture content low and adding salt. Under Napoleon, the French realized that heating certain foods and sealing them in glass jars made them stay fresh longer. United States folklore about the origins of the term "Uncle Sam" includes references to food preservation, including the salted meat that the patriot soldier received from the federal government from an Uncle Sam Wilson's Provision Company that supposedly sent barrels of salt-preserved pork to the troops.

Today, we still use some of these techniques. For instance, pickling vegetables is really a form of using salt for preservation since the *brine* of pickling is a salt solution. We also have *chemical additives* which help preserve food far longer than ancient techniques. The positive impact of food preservation includes the reduction of *food-borne illnesses* and a longer lasting food supply. The negatives include the *ingestion* of chemical additives that may cause reactions in people with food sensitivities or long-term effects that have yet been undetermined. However, certain chemicals are used today because they are considered safe by the Federal Drug Administration and prevent diseases that would otherwise arise from eating spoiled food. For instance, *sodium benzoate* is the sodium salt of benzoic acid, which lowers the *pH* of a food, thus preserving it. Sodium benzoate is used in jams, relishes, dressings, pie and pastry fillings, and even olives. Another example of a chemical preservative is a *sorbate*, the salt version of *sorbic acid*, which has antimicrobial properties and is used in cheeses, sour cream, margarine, and mayonnaise, to name a few items.

In this experiment, you will test the use of salt and sugar as preservatives, comparing them to a *control* with no preservative.

Time Needed

45 minutes to prepare, 10 days to complete

What You Need

- 2 chicken bullion cubes
- hot water, 17 ounces (oz) (500 milliliters [ml])
- pot
- stirring spoon
- 3 glass jars
- scale
- salt, 2 teaspoons (tsp) (10 grams [g])
- sugar, 2 tsp (10 g)
- 12 petri dishes with agar (can be purchased from a science supply company, e.g., Science Kit® & Boreal® Laboratories or Carolina Scientific Supply Company)
- 3 medicine droppers
- black permanent marker

Safety Precautions

Please review and follow the safety guidelines at the beginning of this volume.

What You Do

1. Dissolve both bullion cubes in the pot with hot water. Do not use boiling water.

2. Carefully pour equal amounts of the chicken broth into each of the 3 glass jars (Figure 1).

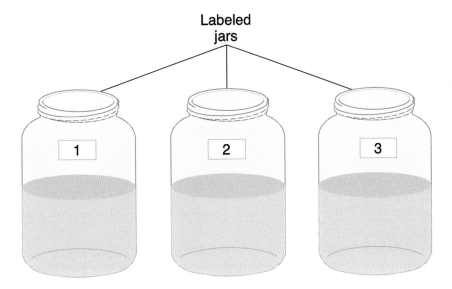

Figure 1

3. Label the jars 1, 2, and 3, respectively (Figure 1).

4. Set jar 1 aside. This will be your control.

5. Add 10 g of salt to the jar 2.

6. Add 10 g of sugar to jar 3.

7. Using a medicine dropper, place a few drops of the solution from jar 1 on the agar of a petri dish.

8. Label the petri dish "jar 1, day 1" (Figure 2).

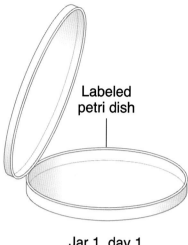

Jar 1, day 1

Figure 2

9. Clean the medicine dropper and set it near jar 1.

10. Repeat steps 7 to 9 with jars 2 and 3, labeling the petri dishes accordingly.

11. After 3 days, record on the data table what you observe in the petri dish.

12. Repeat steps 7 to 11 on the third day after making the solution; on the fifth day; and on the seventh day, labeling the petri dishes accordingly.

Data Table				
Jar	Day 1 dish	Day 3 dish	Day 5 dish	Day 7 dish
1				
2				
3				

 **Observations**

1. Did anything grow on the agar of any of the petri dishes from jar 1? If so, how many days did it take for the growth?

2. Did the sugar or salt prevent or delay the growth of any bacteria on the agar (results of jars 2 and 3)? How do you know?

3. Why are food preservatives important?

4. How can some preservatives be harmful to our health?

Our Findings

Please refer to the Our Findings appendix at the back of this volume.

Further Reading

"Egyptian Food." *KingTut.org.uk.* 2009. Available online. URL: http://www.king-tut.org.uk/ancient-egyptians/egyptian-food.htm. Accessed December 1, 2010. Information about ancient Egyptian food and ancient food preservation techniques.

"Food Additives." 2010. Available online. URL: http://www.foodadditivesworld.com/preservatives.html. Accessed December 1, 2010. Links to explanations on chemical preservatives. Includes a list of common food preservatives.

"Food Preservation." *The Columbia Encyclopedia,* 6th ed. 2008. Available online. URL: http://www.encyclopedia.com/doc/1E1-foodpres.html. Accessed December 1, 2010. Includes a history of food preservation and how food spoilage is prevented.

Minich, Deanna. *An A–Z Guide to Food Additives: Never Eat What You Can't Pronounce*. Newburyport, MA: Conari Press, 2009. Comprehensive listing of food additives, along with tips for people with food allergies and food sensitivities.

National Center for Home Food Preservation. 2010. Available online. URL: http://www.uga.edu/nchfp/. Accessed December 1, 2010. Includes links to publications and processes for preserving food on your own.

15. COMPARING DIFFERENT BRANDS OF BOTTLED WATER

Introduction

Water is considered one of our most important *resources*. It is necessary for *life processes.* Our bodies are made up largely of water. You must *drink* water daily to maintain good health. In most homes, water is readily available from the kitchen or bathroom faucet. The local agencies that provide tap water to your home are required to disclose the results of any test for *contaminants* it conducts. The agencies are also required to maintain strict safety standards. But, due to the public's concerns over contaminants that may still be in tap water, companies selling bottled water are able to charge high prices. The bottled-water industry tries to convince us that its products are *purified* beyond the level of our local tap water. The truth is, some bottled water actually comes from tap water, while other brands may contain more *impurities* than the water from your tap.

In this experiment, you will test and compare different brands of bottled water for quality, as well as compare them to the water quality of your own tap water.

Time Needed

2 hours

What You Need

✎ water quality test kit (available from science supply companies and some home improvement stores, e.g., Science Kit® & Boreal® Laboratories, Carolina Scientific Supply Company, or Orchard Supply Hardware)

✎ bottled water, 1 bottle each of 3 different brands

✎ water purification filter (the type that fits onto the kitchen faucet, available at home improvement stores, e.g., Lowe's or Home Depot)

✎ source of tap water, such as the kitchen sink

✎ pen or pencil

✎ 5 large plastic cups

✎ black marker

 ## Safety Precautions

Please review and follow the safety guidelines at the beginning of this volume.

What You Do

1. Using the black marker, label 3 of the plastic cups with the names of the brands of the bottled water you are testing (Figure 1).

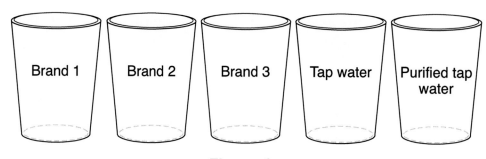

Figure 1

2. Fill each cup with the respective brand of water.
3. Label a fourth cup "tap water" (Figure 1).
4. Fill this cup from the faucet.
5. Label the fifth cup "purified tap water" (Figure 1).
6. Attach the purification filter to the faucet.
7. Fill the fifth cup with the purified water from the tap.

8. Using the water test kit, test for the following qualities or substances: alkalinity, pH, water hardness, free chlorine, total chlorine, total dissolved solids, and dissolved metals.

9. Fill in the brand names of the bottled water you tested on the data table.

10. Complete the data table using the results of the test kit.

Data Table							
Water	**Alkalinity**	**pH**	**Water hardness**	**Free chlorine**	**Total chlorine**	**Total dissolved solids**	**Dissolved metals**
Brand 1 (name)							
Brand 2 (name)							
Brand 3 (name)							
Tap water							
Purified tap water							

 Observations

1. Was there a major difference in the results of the tap water and the purified tap water?

2. Did any of the bottled water brands contain higher levels of chlorine, dissolved solids, or dissolved metals than the tap water? If so, which ones?

3. Did any of the bottled water brands have results so similar to the tap water that a person might infer that the bottled water may be tap water?

4. How do these findings affect your decision to drink tap water or bottled water?

Our Findings

Please refer to the Our Findings appendix at the back of this volume.

Further Reading

"EPA Water News." 2010. U.S. Environmental Protection Agency. Available online. URL: http://www.epa.gov/ow/. Accessed December 1, 2010. Official U.S. government Web site with links to the latest articles on water and water purity.

"FDA Regulates the Safety of Bottled Water Beverages, Including Flavored Water and Nutrient-Added Water Beverages." 2009. Available online. URL: http://www.fda.gov/Food/ResourcesForYou/Consumers/ucm046894.htm. Accessed December 1, 2010. An overview from the Federal Drug Administration about the bottled-water industry.

Royte, Elizabeth. *Bottlemania: Big Business, Local Springs, and the Battle Over America's Drinking Water*. New York: Bloomsbury USA, 2009. About the bottled-water industry, including the environmental impact of plastic bottles.

Stinchfield, Kate. 2009. "Is Your Bottled Water Safe?" Available online. URL: http://www.cnn.com/2009/HEALTH/07/13/bottled.water.safety/index.html. Accessed December 1, 2010. Article from the cable news network CNN's Web site reporting on the possible safety issues of bottled water.

"Water Resources of the United States." 2010. USGS. Available online. URL: http://water.usgs.gov/. Accessed December 1, 2010. Information from the U.S. Geological Survey's Web site about the nation's water resources, including maps and water events.

16. CREATING A LIFE MAP

Introduction

You may have read an *autobiography,* which is a true story that someone writes about his or her own life. You may even have written an autobiography as a school assignment. However, in order to better understand the impact that certain events have in our lives, it is sometimes beneficial to *evaluate* these influences by looking at a visual display. A life map is a series of *symbols* that serve as a *graphic organizer* of your life. Life maps can be used to help set goals, *analyze* the influences in your life, or help you write an autobiography. No words are used in life maps, so all events, people, and influences are represented with symbols.

In this activity, you will recall events and influences in your life, create symbols for them, and draw your own life map.

Time Needed

2 to 3 hours

What You Need

✎ index cards, 1 pack

✎ pen or pencil

✎ set of colored markers, crayons, or pencils

✎ large white posterboard, any size

Safety Precautions

Please review and follow the safety guidelines at the beginning of this volume.

What You Do

1. Write the date of your birth on an index card and note that the event was your birth (Figure 1).

> March 30, 1997
> Born in Los Angeles, California

Figure 1

2. Think about events that have happened in your life since then. Examples of such events are the birth of a *sibling*, starting school, playing in your first sports game, attending a play, visiting an amusement park, moving to the next grade level, or changing schools.

3. Write down each event on a separate index card.

4. Think about goals you have had in your life and about people or events that influence those goals.

5. Write about each of these on a separate index card.

6. Arrange all of the cards in chronological order or in an order that makes sense to you.

7. On the back of each card, make a symbol to represent the event, goal, or person. For instance, the birth of a sister could be represented by a drawing of a baby girl. A teacher who

influenced you might be represented by an apple. Joining a team sport might be represented by a piece of equipment from that sport (Figure 2).

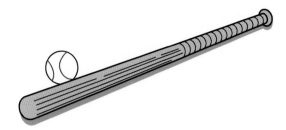

Figure 2

8. On the large posterboard—using colored markers, pencils, or crayons—draw only the symbols that represent the events, goals, and influences of your life. Show the symbols in chronological order or in the direction of influence by using arrows (Figure 3).

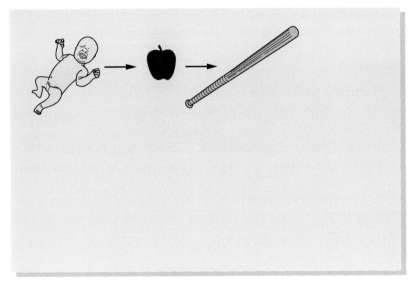

Figure 3

 **Observations**

1. Show your life map to a friend or family member. Can they figure out what you considered to be the major events, people, and influences in your life so far?

2. Did you notice that there were several major events or influences around the same time? If so, how do you think they affected you?

3. How do you think this map might look in 3 years? In 5 years? In 10 years?

Our Findings

Please refer to the Our Findings appendix at the back of this volume.

Further Reading

Drabble, Margaret, and Jenny Stringer. "Autobiography." *The Concise Oxford Companion to English Literature*. 2003. Available online. URL: http://www.encyclopedia.com/doc/1054-autobiography.html. Accessed December 1, 2010. Explanation of what an autobiography is.

"Graphic Organizers." *Graphic.org*. 2010. Available online. URL: http://www.graphic.org/. Accessed December 1, 2010. Contains links to templates for various types of graphic organizers.

———. North Central Regional Educational Laboratory. 1988. Available online. URL: http://www.ncrel.org/sdrs/areas/issues/students/learning/lr1grorg.htm. Accessed December 1, 2010. Explains what a graphic organizer is, how it can be used for organizing thoughts, and examples of graphic organizers.

Signs and Symbols. New York: DK Adult, 2008. Fully illustrated book with explanations and history behind various symbols.

"Symbol." *The Columbia Encyclopedia,* 6th ed. 2008. Available online. URL: http://www.encyclopedia.com. Accessed December 1, 2010. Encyclopedia entry explaining what a symbol is and how symbols are used.

17. EVALUATING THE SUGAR CONTENT OF POPULAR DRINKS

Introduction

Sugar is commonly used to sweeten food and drinks. Sometimes sugar is listed as an ingredient on food labels as *sucrose, lactose,* or *fructose*. It is important to read the nutritional labels and list of ingredients in foods and drinks closely in order to be aware of the amount of sugar you *ingest* daily. This is especially important for people trying to limit *caloric intake* and *blood sugar levels*. Excessive intake of sugar can lead to *obesity*, tooth decay, and *diabetes*. Sometimes, we are already aware that food or drinks—such as cakes, cookies, and sodas—contain sugar. However, there are some types of food and drinks that many people assume are healthy and may not realize that they are ingesting a large amount of sugar.

In this experiment, you will not only compare the amounts of sugar found in sodas, popular sports drinks, and vitamin water but also consider the impact on health.

Time Needed

45 minutes

What You Need

- 2 cans or bottles of regular soda (not diet soda), 1 from each of 2 brands

- 2 bottles of sports drink (e.g., Gatorade® and Powerade®), 1 from each of 2 brands

- 2 bottles of vitamin drinks, 1 from each of 2 brands

✎   triple-beam balance, (see page 98, Figure 3)

✎   1 bag of granulated sugar

✎   6 small plates

✎   pen or pencil

✎   small spoon

 Safety Precautions

Please review and follow the safety guidelines at the beginning of this volume.

What You Do

1. Read the nutritional information on one of the sports drinks. Note the sugar content per serving and the number of servings per container. Figure 1 shows an example of a label with nutritional information.

Nutrition Facts		
Serving Size 8 oz Serving per container 2		
Amount Per Serving		
Calories 155	Calories from Fat 93	
		% Daily Value*
Total Fat 11g		**16%**
Saturated Fat 3g		**15%**
Trans Fat		
Cholesterol 0mg		**0%**
Sodiun 148mg		**6%**
Total Carbohydrate 14g		**5%**
Dietary Fiber 1g		**5%**
Sugars 1g		
Protein 2g		
Vitamin A 0% Vitamin C 9% Calcium 1% Iron 3%		
*Percent Daily Values are based on a 2,000 calorie diet. Your daily values may be higher or lower depending on your calorie needs.		

Figure 1

2. Record on the data table the amount of sugar in the container.

3. Repeat steps 1 and 2 for each of the other drinks.

4. Using the triple-beam balance, measure the same amount of granulated sugar as that found in the first drink.

5. Place the sugar on the first plate (Figure 2).

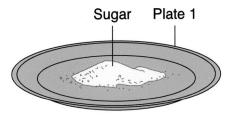

Figure 2

6. Repeat steps 4 and 5 for each of the drinks and place the mounds on sugar on individual plates (Figure 3).

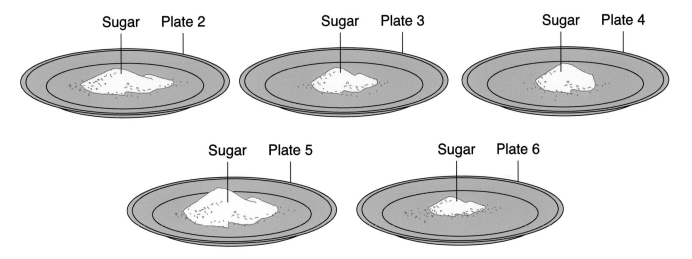

Figure 3

Data Table			
Drink	Sugar per serving	Serving per container	Total sugar per container (sugar per serving x servings per container)
Water	0	N/A	0
Sports drink 1			
Sports drink 2			
Soda 1			
Soda 2			
Vitamin drink 1			
Vitamin drink 2			

 **Observations**

1. Which drink had the most sugar? Which had the least?
2. Were you surprised by the amount of sugar in the sports drink? Why or why not?
3. Plain water contains zero sugar. How did the vitamin drinks compare to plain water in their sugar content?

4. What impact do you think the sugar content of these has on the health of people who drink them? Do you think most people are aware of the sugar content?

Our Findings

Please refer to the Our Findings appendix at the back of this volume.

Further Reading

Appleton, Nancy, and G. N. Jacobs. *Suicide by Sugar: A Startling Look at Our #1 National Addiction*. Garden City Park, NY: Square One Publishers, 2009. An honest look at the health problems caused by the nation's intake of large amounts of sugar.

"Fructose." *The Columbia Encyclopedia,* 6th ed. 2008. Available online. URL: http://www.encyclopedia.com/doc/1E1-fructose.html. Accessed December 1, 2010. Short entry explaining what fructose is and how it is made.

Gatorade.com. 2010. Available online. URL: http://www.gatorade.com. Accessed December 1, 2010. Official Web site of the sports drink Gatorade,® including nutritional information.

Goodhue, David. AllHeadlineNews.com. 2010. "Researchers Say Sugar-Sweetened Sports Drinks Causing More Diabetes Cases." Available online. URL: http://www.allheadlinenews.com/articles/7018033393. Accessed December 1, 2010. Article about the hidden epidemic of diabetes now linked to sports drinks that many children and parents assume are healthy to drink.

Ruhl, Jenny. *Blood Sugar 101: What They Don't Tell You About Diabetes*. Turners Falls, MA: Technion Books, 2008. Research in layman's terms regarding the impact of blood sugar on diabetes.

18. STUDYING CONSUMERISM IN TELEVISION COMMERCIALS

Introduction

The *marketing industry* is constantly looking for new audiences to buy products. One of the latest developments in advertising has been the targeting of *tweens* and teenagers. Tweens are those who are not little children but have not yet reached their teenage years. They are eager to dress, look, and act like their *adolescent* counterparts. Teenagers are already a mass market for advertisers, so this audience for certain products may not have grown considerably. By treating teenagers and pre-adolescents as mature *consumers*, advertisers have bypassed parents and capitalized on the need of adolescents and tweens to be perceived as "cool." This audience is willing to pay top dollar to buy products that will make them the *trendsetters*. Advertisers often appeal to this age group's attitudes and concerns toward *body image*, physical appeal, and popularity.

In this activity, you will examine marketing in the media geared toward tweens and teenagers and analyze the methods used to persuade them to purchase products.

Time Needed

about 3 hours

What You Need

- ✎ pen or pencil
- ✎ paper, a few sheets, lined or unlined
- ✎ magazines that you can cut, ideally those for teens or fashion magazines (e.g., *Seventeen*)

- large, white posterboard, any size
- glue stick
- scissors
- television set

Safety Precautions

Please review and follow the safety guidelines at the beginning of this volume. Parental involvement in choosing television shows is recommended.

What You Do

1. Watch one or more television shows geared toward teens or tweens.
2. Pay careful attention to the commercials shown during those shows.
3. Show on the data table your comments about the commercials.
4. Look through the magazines and pay careful attention to the advertisements.
5. Cut out the ads you believe are targeted toward teen or tween body image, popularity, or physical appeal (Figure 1).

Figure 1

6. Glue the ads on a posterboard.

7. Observe the montage you have made and look for patterns.

Data Table			
What time was the commercial on?	What was the product being sold?	What age group do you think was targeted?	What methods were used to persuade you to purchase the product?

 Observations

1. Did you find any patterns to the type of products being sold through commercials?

2. What methods did the advertisers use most to persuade you to purchase their products?

3. What patterns did you find in the magazine ads for methods of persuading you to purchase the products?

4. What types of products were being marketed the most in the ads you found?

5. Do you think you are easily persuaded by these methods?

6. Do you view commercials and magazine ads any differently now that you are aware that the advertisers are trying to target you?

Our Findings

Please refer to the Our Findings appendix at the back of this volume.

Further Reading

"Body Image." U.S. Department of Health and Human Services. 2009. Available online. URL: http://www.womenshealth.gov/bodyimage/. Accessed December 1, 2010. Official government Web site devoted to women's health issues, with an article about how women perceive their own body image.

Dunham, Deb. *Tween You and Me: A Pre-Teen Guide to Becoming Your Best Self*. Maroochydore, Australia: Empowered Publishing, 2009. A guide for tweens on how to deal with the issues relevant to that age group and how to survive those turbulent years.

"Propaganda Techniques." *Thinkquest*. 2001. Available online. URL: http://library.thinkquest.org/C0111500/proptech.htm. Accessed December 1, 2010. Describes several techniques used in advertising to persuade an audience to purchase products or services.

Tween.com. 2010. Available online. URL: http://www.tween.com/. Accessed December 1, 2010. Commercial Web site dedicated to tween topics, links, and media.

Wykes, Maggie, and Barrie Gunter. *The Media and Body Image: If Looks Could Kill*. Newbury Park, CA: Sage Publications, 2005. Discusses the impact of the media on body image and eating disorders.

19. COMPARING IRON IN BREAKFAST CEREALS

Introduction

Iron is essential for many of the *proteins* and *enzymes* necessary to maintain good health in the human body. Iron is needed for the *hemoglobin* of blood cells. The iron allows *oxygen* to bind to the blood cells, then the blood cells deliver this oxygen throughout the body. Iron *deficiency* causes people to become easily *fatigued* because their blood cannot deliver the amount of oxygen needed. Iron is found naturally in red meat, eggs, seafood, and poultry. Red meat is thought to be richest in iron. Iron is also found in *supplements* such as *multivitamins* and is often added to foods like breakfast cereals.

In this experiment, you will compare different breakfast cereals to determine if the same amounts of these cereals provide the human body with equal amounts of iron.

Time Needed

45 minutes

What You Need

- 3 different brands of breakfast cereals that are served cold (e.g., Frosted Flakes®, Wheaties®, Total®)
- 3 Ziploc® baggies, sandwich size
- measuring cup
- bar magnet, at least 3 inches (7.62 centimeters [cm]) long, any color except gray or black
- pen or pencil

- ✎ 3 small bowls
- ✎ triple-beam balance
- ✎ hot water, 3 cups (700 milliliters [ml])
- ✎ 3 wooden mixing spoons
- ✎ clock or watch

 ## Safety Precautions

Please review and follow the safety guidelines at the beginning of this volume.

What You Do

1. Pour 1 cup (237 ml) of the first brand of cereal into a Ziploc® bag.
2. Securely seal the bag.
3. Using your hands, crush the cereal flakes as finely as you can.
4. Pour the crushed flakes into bowl 1.
5. Repeat steps 1 through 4 with the second and third brands of cereal, and pour the crushed flakes into bowls 2 and 3, respectively (Figure 1).

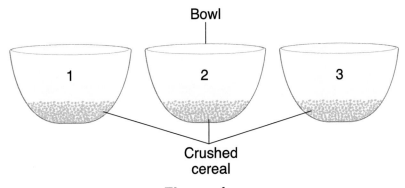

Bowl

Crushed cereal

Figure 1

6. Add 1 cup of hot water to the first bowl and carefully mix with a wooden spoon.

7. Remove the spoon and stir the mixture with the bar magnet instead (Figure 2).

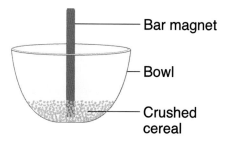

Bar magnet

Bowl

Crushed cereal

Figure 2

8. Continue stirring for 5 minutes.
9. Remove the magnet from the mixture.
10. Scrape the iron filings that have attached to the magnet onto the triple-beam balance (Figure 3).

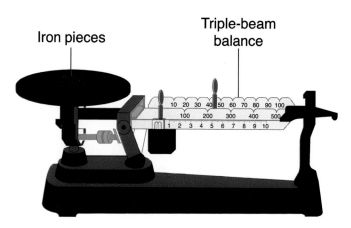

Iron pieces

Triple-beam balance

Figure 3

11. Weigh the iron.
12. Record the weight on the data table.
13. Remove the pieces of iron from the balance.
14. Repeat steps 6 to 13 with bowls 2 and 3.

Data Table	
Brand of cereal	**Weight of iron pieces**

 **Observations**

1. Did all 3 cereals contain the same amount of iron per cup of cereal?

2. Why is iron important for the human body?

3. Iron is added to cereals. What other foods are natural sources of iron?

Our Findings

Please refer to the Our Findings appendix at the back of this volume.

Further Reading

"Anemia." *The Columbia Encyclopedia,* 6th ed. 2008. Available online. URL: http://www.encyclopedia.com/doc/1E1-anemia.html. Accessed December 1, 2010. Discusses the causes and symptoms of anemia.

Fillon, Mike. *Real RDAs for Real People: Why "Official" Nutrition Guidelines Aren't Enough and What to Do About It*. Salt Lake City: Woodland Publishing, 2003. This book points out that simply following recommended daily allowances of certain foods, vitamins, and minerals may not be enough to maintain good health since all individuals have different needs.

"Hemoglobin." *The Columbia Encyclopedia,* 6th ed. 2008. Available online. URL: http://www.encyclopedia.com/doc/1E1-hemoglob.html. Accessed December 1, 2010. Entry about hemoglobin and how it binds to oxygen.

"Iron and Anemia." *Rutgers.* 2005. Available online. URL: http://health.rutgers.edu/factsheets/iron.htm. Accessed December 1, 2010. Article containing information about the anemia resulting from iron deficiency.

Muzaurieta, Annie. "Top-10 Real Food Sources of Iron." 2010. Available online. URL: http://www.thedailygreen.com/healthy-eating/eat-safe/top-iron-sources-44111008. Accessed December 1, 2010. Web site with up-to-date information and blogs concerning health and environmental issues. Includes a list of the foods containing the most iron.

20. THE SPREAD OF INFECTION

Introduction

Infections in people can be caused by various types of *viruses or bacteria*. They may be spread when an uninfected person touches an infected person, such as a person with a cold who has just coughed into his or her hand before shaking hands. Then the uninfected person may rub his or her eyes, allowing the infection to enter through the tear ducts. Another way for infection to spread is through food handling. If a person with infectious *body fluids* on his or hands does not wash his hands thoroughly and then touches food, the infection can be *ingested* along with the food. Some infections are spread by direct contact of bodily fluids. You can prevent the spread of infection by being careful: Always wash your hands thoroughly, avoid rubbing your eyes after shaking hands with someone who has a cold, cook food thoroughly, refrigerate foods that need to be kept cool, and avoid direct contact with someone else's body fluids.

In this experiment, you will *simulate* the spread of infection through the contact of bodily fluids.

Time Needed

40 minutes

What You Need

- 9 plastic cups
- water, enough to fill all of the cups about 1/3 full
- water softener (such as Calgon®) enough to turn 1 cup of water to a pH of 10

10 pH indicator papers, with accompanying color chart for pH (see Figure 1)

✎ black permanent marker

Safety Precautions

Please review and follow the safety guidelines at the beginning of this volume. Make sure to wear goggles when handling chemicals.

What You Do

1. In one cup, pour enough water to fill the cup about 1/3 to 1/2 full.

2. Add water softener to the cup until a pH indicator strip dipped into the water shows the color indicating a pH of 10 (Figure 1).

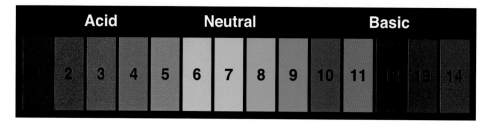

Figure 1

3. Label the other cups 1 to 8.

4. Pour some of your basic solution into cup 1, enough to fill the cup 1/3 full. This represents the body fluids of an infected person.

5. Fill the other 7 cups 1/3 full with water. These represent people who have not yet been infected by a disease.

6. Test the pH of one of the cups of water as a baseline. Record the pH of the water on the data table.

7. Pour the contents of cup 1 into cup 2 (Figure 2).

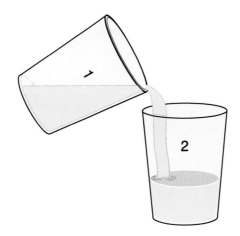

Figure 2

8. Pour half the current contents of cup 2 back into cup 1.

9. Pour the contents of cup 1 into cup 3.

10. Pour half the current contents of cup 3 back into cup 1.

11. Pour the contents of cup 2 into cup 4.

12. Pour half the current contents of cup 4 back into cup 2.

13. Pour the contents of cups 1, 2, 3, and 4 into cups 5, 6, 7, and 8, respectively (Figure 3).

Figure 3

14. Pour half the current contents of cups 5, 6, 7, and 8 back into cups 1, 2, 3, and 4, respectively.

15. Test cups 1 through 8 with pH indicator paper.

16. Record the pH of each cup on the data table.

Data Table: pH 10 of basic solution; pH of water: _____	
Cup	pH
1	
2	
3	
4	
5	
6	
7	
8	

 Observations

1. Did the pH levels of the cups change after they were mixed with the contents of other cups?
2. How does this experiment simulate the spread of infection?
3. What can be done to prevent the spread of infectious diseases?

Our Findings

Please refer to the Our Findings appendix at the back of this volume.

Further Reading

"Bacteria." *The Columbia Encyclopedia,* 6th ed. 2008. March 9, 2010. Available online. URL: http://www.encyclopedia.com/doc/1E1-bacteria.html. Accessed December 1, 2010. Defines bacteria, providing examples of types of bacteria and explaining their role in disease.

cdc.gov. Centers for Disease Control and Prevention. 2010. Available online. URL: http://www.cdc.gov/. Accessed December 1, 2010. This official government Web site of the Centers for Disease Control includes information on the spread and prevention of infectious diseases.

Clarke, John Henry. *Cold Catching, Cold Preventing, Cold Curing.* Whitefish, MT: Kessinger Publishing, 2009. Explaining how you catch a cold, how to prevent a cold, and how to reduce the symptoms of a cold.

"Infectious Diseases." *MayoClinic.com.* 2009. Available online. URL: http://www.mayoclinic.com/health/infectious-diseases/DS01145. Accessed December 1, 2010. Information from the Mayo Clinic defining infectious diseases and symptoms, and how to prevent the spread of such diseases.

"Virus." *The Columbia Encyclopedia,* 6th ed. 2008. Available online. URL: http://www.encyclopedia.com/doc/1E1-virus.html. Accessed December 1, 2010. About viruses: what they are and how they cause diseases.

Scope and Sequence Chart

This chart is aligned with the National Science Content Standards. Each state may have its own specific content standards, so please refer to your local and state content standards for additional information. As always, adult supervision is recommended (or required in some instances), and discretion should be used in selecting experiments appropriate for each age group or individual children.

Unifying Concepts and Processes	all
Science as Inquiry	all
Physical Science	
Properties of objects and materials	
Properties and changes of properties in matter	
Position and motion of objects	
Motions and forces	
Light, heat, electricity, and magnetism	
Transfer of energy	
Life Science	
Structure and function in living systems	4, 5, 6
Life cycles of organisms	16
Reproduction and heredity	
Regulation and behavior	1, 2, 3, 4, 5, 6, 18, 20
Organisms and environments	

Populations and ecosystems	
Diversity and adaptations of organisms	
Earth Science	
Properties of Earth materials	
Structure of the Earth system	
Objects in the sky	
Changes in Earth and sky	
Earth's history	
Earth in the solar system	
Science and Technology	
Science in Personal and Social Perspectives	all
Personal health	all
Characteristics and changes in populations	
Types of resources	
Changes in environments	
Science and technology in local challenges	18, 20
Populations, resources, and environments	
Natural hazards	
Risks and benefits	1, 2, 3, 7, 8, 9, 10, 11, 12, 14, 17
Science and technology in society	13, 14, 15, 17, 18, 19
History and Nature of Science	all

Grade Level

Setting

The experiments are classified by materials and equipment use as follows:

- Those under SCHOOL LABORATORY involve materials and equipment found only in science laboratories. Those under SCHOOL LABORATORY must be carried out there under the supervision of the teacher or another adult.

- Those under HOME involve household or everyday materials. Some of these can be done at home, but call for supervision.

- The experiments classified under OUTDOORS may be done at the school or at the home, but require access to outdoor areas and call for supervision.

SCHOOL LABORATORY

13. Comparing Vitamin-C Content
17. Evaluating the Sugar Content of Popular Drinks

HOME

1. Eating Healthy and Fitness Plan

2. Healthy Food Choices

3. Self-Esteem

4. Taking Blood Pressure

5. Taking a Pulse at Multiple Sites

6. Studying Nerves—Sensitivity Testing

7. Simulating the Negative Effects of Tobacco—Part 1

8. Simulating the Negative Effects of Tobacco—Part 2

9. Tooth Care—Part 1: Fluoride

10. Tooth Care—Part 2: Tooth Decay

11. Modeling Blood Alcohol Content

12. Evaluating Stressors

OUTDOORS

N/A

Our Findings

1. EATING HEALTHY AND FITNESS PLAN

1. Answers will vary.

2. Answers will vary.

3. Answers will vary.

4. Answers will vary.

5. Answers will vary but may include parents, teachers, coaches, doctors, and friends.

2. HEALTHY FOOD CHOICES

1. Answers will vary.

2. Answers will vary.

3. Answers will vary.

3. SELF-ESTEEM

1. Answers will vary.

2. Answers will vary.

3. Answers will vary.

4. Answers will vary but may include that people are individuals and that no two people are the same.

4. TAKING BLOOD PRESSURE

1. Answers will vary.

2. 140/90 and over is considered high blood pressure; normal blood pressure is under 120/80.

3. Answers will vary but may include that tracking blood pressure can prevent certain types of conditions and diagnosing illnesses.

5. TAKING A PULSE AT MULTIPLE SITES

1. Answers will vary.

2. Answers will vary.

3. Answers will vary but may include when there has been a major injury to the hand or arm, when the wrist is inaccessible, or if someone is missing an arm.

4. Your pulse rate is a reflection of your heart beat, so your pulse rate is how many times your heart beats.

6. STUDYING NERVES—SENSITIVITY TESTING

1. Answers will vary but will most likely be the fingertips; ability to sense the difference between the ends of the paper clips when close together.

2. Answers will vary but will most likely be the upper arm or forearm; difficulty sensing the paper clips as 2 separate points.

3. It is important to have more receptors in the parts of the hand you use to touch, sense pressure, or sense heat so that you can hold objects and prevent burns.

4. Mapping nerve sensitivity could determine if the person has damaged nerves that could affect a person's ability to use that part of the body even if, on the outside, the person appears uninjured or healed.

7. SIMULATING THE NEGATIVE EFFECTS OF TOBACCO—PART 1

1. The pump represents the lungs. Tobacco puts a strain on the lungs and makes it difficult to breathe.

2. The thinner straws make it more difficult to take up the water. When blood vessels constrict, it becomes more difficult to pump blood through them and get blood to all the parts of your body.

3. Based on the simulation, your body absorbs poisonous carbon monoxide more quickly than air.

8. SIMULATING THE NEGATIVE EFFECTS OF TOBACCO—PART 2

1. Answers will vary.

2. The water flowed slower through the molasses-covered filter.

3. Tar builds up in the lungs just as the molasses coated the filter. This makes it harder for the lungs to take in enough air.

9. TOOTH CARE—PART 1: FLUORIDE

1. The X on the untreated side started to fade.

2. The side not treated was soft to the touch and could be pushed in, while the treated side was still hard.

3. The fluoride protected one-half of the egg.

4. Fluoride can form a protective covering over your teeth, protecting them from tooth decay.

10. TOOTH CARE—PART 2: TOOTH DECAY

1. Flossing was more effective.

2. Only flossing can effectively remove certain particles from specific areas in between your teeth.

3. Tooth decay will occur between teeth where the brush cannot reach.

4. Answers will vary.

5. The sugars will promote tooth decay because the sugars will be allowed to stay, promoting bacterial growth and plaque.

11. MODELING BLOOD ALCOHOL CONTENT

1. Answers will vary but should show that when a person is impaired, the beanbags were dropped more frequently.

2. If impaired by alcohol, you are more likely to make mistakes when driving and will be unable to drive safely.

3. Answers will vary.

4. Answers will vary.

12. EVALUATING STRESSORS

1. Answers will vary.

2. Answers will vary.

3. Answers will vary.

4. Stress wears the body down and leaves you susceptible to illness.

13. COMPARING VITAMIN-C CONTENT

1. Answers will vary, but whichever had the lightest color had a higher vitamin-C content.

2. Answers will vary, but may include that they contained different amounts of vitamin C.

3. Answers will vary depending on results of experiment.

14. FOOD PRESERVATION

1. Answers will vary.

2. Answers will vary but should include that, yes, there was less or no bacterial growth.

3. Food preservatives allow food to last longer, prevent spoilage, prevent certain diseases caused by food that has spoiled, and makes food more accessible because it can be transported over distances without going bad.

4. Answers will vary but may include that some preservatives contain chemicals harmful to human health or that some people may be allergic to the preservative.

15. COMPARING DIFFERENT BRANDS OF BOTTLED WATER

1. Answers will vary.

2. Answers will vary.

3. Answers will vary.

4. Answers will vary.

16. CREATING A LIFE MAP

1. Answers will vary.

2. Answers will vary.

3. Answers will vary.

17. EVALUATING THE SUGAR CONTENT OF POPULAR DRINKS

1. Answers will vary.

2. Answers will vary.

3. Answers will vary but may include that vitamin water contained sugar while plain water did not.

4. Answers will vary but may include that people do not realize they are taking in additional sugar, which can lead to weight gain and tooth decay.

18. STUDYING CONSUMERISM IN TELEVISION COMMERCIALS

1. Answers will vary.

2. Answers will vary.

3. Answers will vary.

4. Answers will vary.

5. Answers will vary.

6. Answers will vary.

19. COMPARING IRON IN BREAKFAST CEREALS

1. Answers will vary.

2. Iron is needed for the hemoglobin in your blood cells. The iron allows oxygen to bind to the blood cells, then the blood cells deliver this oxygen throughout the human body.

3. Iron is found naturally in red meat, eggs, seafood, and poultry.

20. THE SPREAD OF INFECTION

1. Yes.

2. Infections are passed from person to person, just as the pH of the water changed when "infected."

3. Some of the actions you can take to prevent the spread of infection include: always wash your hands thoroughly, avoid rubbing your eyes after shaking hands with someone who has a cold, cook food thoroughly, refrigerate foods that need to be kept cool, and avoid direct contact with someone else's body fluids.

Tips for Teachers

General

- Always review all safety guidelines before attempting any experiment.
- Enforce all safety guidelines.
- Try the experiment on your own first to be better prepared for possible questions that may arise.
- You may try demonstrating each step of the experiment as you explain it to the students.
- Check for correlation to standards in order to best match the experiment to the curriculum.
- Provide adult assistance and supervision. Do not leave students unsupervised.
- Make sure students feel comfortable asking for help when needed.

Equipment and Supplies

- Most glassware can be purchased from scientific supply companies like Carolina Science Supply Company. Many companies have both print and online catalogs.
- Chemicals and special materials can also be purchased from these companies.
- Many of the supplies and substances used in the experiments are household items that can be found at home or purchased at a local market.
- For some of the hard-to-find items (e.g., extra-large jars), try asking local restaurants, or check warehouse-type stores that carry industrial-size items. For some substances (e.g., lamp oil), you should check with hardware or home-improvement stores.

Special-Needs Students

- Please make sure to follow the individualized education plans (IEPs) and 504 accommodation plans for any special-needs students.
- Provide a handout for students who require visual aids.
- Create a graphic representation of the experiment for students who use picture cards to communicate.

(continued)

- For visually disabled students, provide copies with enlarged print.
- Involve students with dexterity issues by providing opportunities to participate in ways that match their abilities—e.g., be the timekeeper or the instruction reader.
- Read aloud directions for students who require verbal cues.
- Record the instructions for playback.
- Repeat instructions more than once.
- Demonstrate the experiment so that students can see how it should be done correctly.
- Check frequently for comprehension.
- Ask students to repeat the information so that you can ensure accuracy.
- Break down directions into simple steps.
- Have students work with a lab partner or in a lab group.
- Provide adult assistance when necessary.
- Make sure that students with auditory disabilities know visual cues in case of danger or emergency.
- Simplify the experiment for students with developmental disabilities.
- Incorporate assistive technology for students who require it; e.g., use of Alphasmart® keyboards for recording observations and for dictation software.
- Provide preferred seating (e.g., front row) for students with disabilities to ensure they are able to see and hear demonstrations.
- Provide an interpreter if available for students with auditory disabilities who require American Sign Language.
- Consult with your school's inclusion specialist, resource teacher, or special education teacher for additional suggestions.
- Arrange furniture so that all students have clear access to information being presented and can move about the room (e.g., wheelchair-accessible aisles of about 48 inches).
- Offer students the option of recording their responses.
- Eliminate background noise when it is distracting.
- Face the class when speaking, and keep your face visible for students who lip-read.
- Repeat new words in various contexts to enhance vocabulary.
- Alter table heights for wheelchair access.

(continued)

- Substitute equipment with larger sizes for easy gripping.
- Ask the student if he or she needs help before offering it.
- Place materials within easy reach of the students.
- Be aware of temperature. Some students may not be able to feel heat or cold and might injure themselves.
- Identify yourself to students with visual impairments. Also speak when you enter or leave the room.
- For visually impaired students, give directions in relation to the student's body. Do not use words like "over here." Also describe verbally what is happening in the experiment.

Glossary

A

abdominal aorta	the part of the aorta between the diaphragm and the bifurcation into the right and left common iliac arteries
absorb	to suck up or take in
absorption	the process of absorbing or being absorbed
accumulation	increase or growth by addition; process of accumulating
adolescent	youth, one that is in the state of adolescence
air sacs	thin-walled dilation of trachea
analyze	study or determine by breaking down parts of the subject through observation
antioxidants	oxidation or reactions promoted by oxygen, peroxides, or free radicals
aorta	carries blood from the heart to be distributed by branch arteries through the body
arteries	tubular-branching muscular and elastic-walled vessels that carry blood from the heart through the body
ascertain	to make certain, exact, or precise
autobiography	a history of a person's life, written or told by that same person

B

bacteria	one-celled organisms typically from the Moneran kingdom
benzoic acid	a white, crystalline, slightly water-soluble powder used as a preservative
blood alcohol content	concentration of alcohol in a person's blood
blood pressure	pressure exerted by the blood on the walls of the blood vessels
bloodstream	the flowing blood in a circulatory system
blood sugar levels	amount of glucose present in the blood
blood vessels	arteries that carry blood away from the heart
body fluids	liquids that are inside the bodies of living organisms
body image	a person's perception of his or her own physical appearance
body mass index	a measurement of fat to muscle mass in the body
bone density	a measurement of the mineral density of bone

brachial artery	chief artery of the upper arm
brine	water saturated with salt

C

calcium	component of bone, skeletal mass, and shell; for example, a necessary element in nerve conduction, heartbeat, muscle contraction, and many other physiological functions
calipers	calibrated instruments for measuring thickness or distances
caloric intake	amount of calories an organism takes in
cancer	a malignant and invasive growth or tumor
carbon monoxide	colorless, odorless, poisonous gas
carcinogens	any substance or agent that tends to produce a cancer
cardiovascular	relating to the heart and blood vessels; see **exercise**
carotid artery	large arteries, one on each side of the heart that carry blood to the head
cavities	holes or structural damage in the teeth
central nervous system	brain and spinal cord
chemical additives	chemical materials added into other substances
circulating	cyclical motion, continuously passing from one to another
citrus	edible fruit with firm, usually thick, rind and pulpy flesh
climate	a region of Earth having specific conditions, especially temperature and precipitation
collagen	fibrous proteins involved in connective tissue fibrils; see **fibril**
concentrate	not diluted, extremely dense
concrete	a tangible observation, oftentimes a fact
constrict	to make narrow or draw together
consume	to take in or eat
consumers	individuals who purchase goods and services
contaminant	impurity
control	the controlled variable that does not change
coping	to deal with, to come to terms with

D

deficiency	lacking or inadequacy
dental	cavity formation in teeth caused by bacteria that attach to teeth

dental plaque	build-up of mucus and bacteria on the surface of a tooth
diabetes	disease marked by high levels of sugar in the blood
diastole	period of time when the heart fills with blood after systole
digestion	to process and break down food in the body

E

environment	air, water, minerals, organisms, and all other external factors surrounding and affecting a given organism at any time
enzymes	capable of catalytic action such as digestion
evaluate	to assess a situation carefully
exercise	performing physical actions to increase cardiovascular and muscle function
exhaust	emissions from a car

F

fatigued	extreme tiredness
femoral artery	blood vessel immediately behind the inguinal ligament, midway between the anterior superior spine of the ilium and the symphysis pubis
fibril	neurofibril, hair-thin tissue in nerves
floss	dental accessory, a thin string-like substance, used to clean between teeth and gums
fluoride	a compound of fluorine, used in dentists' offices to clean teeth
food-borne illness	any illness resulting from the consumption of contaminated food
food groups	a method of classification for the various foods that people consume, based on the nutritional properties of these types of foods and their location in a hierarchy of nutrition
food preservation	the process of treating and handling food to stop or greatly slow down spoilage
food pyramid	adopted by the USDA (United States Department of Agriculture) in 1992 to replace the classification system of earlier food groups
fructose	a simple monosaccharide found in many foods

G

ganglia	a biological tissue mass, most commonly a mass of nerve cell bodies
graphic organizer	visual representations of knowledge, concepts, or ideas
gum disease	gingivitis and periodontitis, diseases of the gums

H

hemoglobin   the iron-containing, oxygen-transport metalloprotein in the red blood cells
of vertebrates

hormone   a chemical released by a cell in one part of the body that sends out
messages that affect cells in other parts of the organism

I

imbibe   to consume by drinking

immune system   a system of biological structures and processes within an organism
that protects against disease by identifying and killing pathogens and
tumor cells

impairs   to block or stop from happening

impurities   something that is impure or contaminates something pure

infections   a persistent bacterial infection of some organ or region

ingest   to take in

ingestion   to take in for digestion

inhale   to draw in by breathing

iron   component of hemoglobin that transports oxygen in the blood

L

lactose   disaccharide sugar present in milk and yielding glucose

larynx   upper part of the trachea of air-breathing vertebrates

life processes   procession of occurrences that take place within life cycles

lurking   to lie in wait or concealment

M

marketing industry industry that uses advertising techniques to sell products

minerals   any of a class of inorganic substances occurring in nature with a definite
chemical composition and crystal structure

multivitamin   vitamin compound containing more than one vitamin

N

nerves   one or more bundles of fibers forming part of a system that conveys
impulses of sensation and motion between the brain or spinal cord and
other parts of the body

nervous system   the system of nerves and nerve centers in an animal or human, including
the brain, spinal cord, nerves, and ganglia

neurons	a specialized, impulse-conducting cell that is the functional unit of the nervous system, consisting of the cell body and its processes, the axon and dendrites
nicotine	a colorless, oily, water-soluble, highly toxic, liquid alkaloid found in tobacco and used as an insecticide
nutrition	the act or process of nourishing or being nourished

O

obesity	a condition characterized by the excessive accumulation of fat in the body
optimal	most desirable or satisfactory
oxygen	a colorless, odorless gas present in nature
oxygenated	combined with oxygen

P

particles	tiny fragments
pasteurize	to heat food for a sufficient time so as to destroy microorganisms
peripheral nervous system	connects the central nervous system to the limbs and organs
personal inventory	keeping track of one's data and instruments, etc.
pessimistic	negative aspect of situations
pollen	contains the micro-gametophytes of seed plants
pollution	contamination of the environment
popliteal artery	continuation of the femoral artery
proteins	organic compounds made of amino acids
pulse	arterial palpation of a heartbeat
purified	to make pure, reduce impurities and contaminants

R

radial artery	the main blood vessel with oxygenated blood of the forearm
receptors	nerve cells that mediate certain physiological responses
remineralize	process of restoring minerals
resources	any physical or virtual entity of limited availability
respiratory system	controls oxygen exchange through all parts of the body
risk behaviors	behaviors that put one at risk for negative consequences

S

self-esteem	self-confidence and self-acceptance of oneself
self-perception	the way people perceive themselves
sensory	nerve cells transmitting recognition of the senses
simulate	to create a model of
sodium benzoate	sodium salt of benzoic acid, used as a preservative
sorbate	a salt of sorbic acid
sorbic acid	a white, crystalline compound soluble in organic solvents, used as a preservative
sphygmomano-meter	a device for monitoring blood pressure
spinal cord	elongated bundles of nervous tissues that carry nerve impulses between the brain and the rest of the body
stethoscope	instrument used to listen to sounds produced by the body
stimulation	action of various agents of receptor nerve cells
strain	when a muscle becomes overstretched or tears
stress	frustration, anger, or anxiety caused by situations or thoughts
stressor	agent, condition, or other stimulus that causes stress
stroke	interruption of the blood supply to any part of the brain
substances	material with a specific chemical composition
sucrose	organic compound (sugar) widely used as sweetener or preservative
sufficient	good amount, has reached adequacy
supplements	nutrition substitutes
symbols	representations of something else
systole	rhythmic contraction of the heart when the blood is forced outward

T

tar	toxic chemical found in cigarettes
tobacco	processed from leaves of Nicotiana plants, used in cigarettes
tooth enamel	hard-surface substance on the teeth
trendsetters	people who set fashion, music, and other social matters
tweens	youth ages 11 to 12 years old

V

ventricle	chamber that collects blood from an atrium and pumps it out of the heart

virus   infectious agent, parisitic

vitamin C   ascorbic acid found in citrus fruit, tomatoes, and other foods

W

water soluble   ability to dissolve in water

Internet Resources

The Internet is a wealth of information and resources for students, parents, and teachers. However, all sources should be verified for fact, and it is recommended never to rely on any single source for in-depth research. The following list of resources is a sample of what the World Wide Web has to offer.

Action for Healthy Kids. Available online. URL: http://www.actionforhealthykids.org/. Accessed July 25, 2010. This Web site contains health information for children and programs that can be used in the classroom to encourage good health choices.

Alliance for a Healthier Generation. Available online. URL: http://www.healthiergeneration.org/. Accessed July 25, 2010. Alliance for a Healthier Generation is a program that allows schools to adopt a healthier lifestyle with free resources available to school staff and parents who want to promote a healthier life for their children.

American Alliance for Physical Education, Recreation, and Dance. Available online. URL: http://www.aahperd.org/. Accessed July 25, 2010. The Web site provides access to books to be used in the classroom and provides support for professionals in the physical education field. Scholarships and other recognitions are also available.

American Heart Association. Available online. URL: http: //www.americanheart.org/presenter.jhtml?identifier=1200000. Accessed May 5, 2010. General information from the American Heart Association on how to maintain a healthy heart.

———. "Blood Pressure." Available online. URL: http: //www.americanheart.org/presenter.jhtml?identifier=4473. Accessed May 5, 2010. Provides information about what blood pressure is, as well as what constitutes high and low blood pressure.

Center for Disease Control. "Healthy Youth." Available online. URL: http://apps.nccd.cdc.gov/sher/. Accessed July 25, 2010. This Web site has resources for all age groups and discusses a variety of health topics and includes additional resources for the classroom teacher.

Child Development Institute. "Self-esteem: How to Help children and Teens Develop a Positive Self-Image." Available online. URL: http://www.childdevelopmentinfo.com/parenting/self_esteem.shtml. Accessed July 29, 2010. Parenting Web site that provides practical advice on how to promote positive self-esteem.

Crestkids.com. Available online. URL: http: //www.crestkids.com. Accessed May 5, 2010. Commercial Web site that provides information for children regarding tooth care.

Discovery Education. Available online. URL: http: //www.discoveryschool.com. Accessed May 5, 2010. Informational site that contains lessons and links for educational purposes.

Doherty, Jennifer, and Ingrid Waldron. University of Pennsylvania, 2007. "Teacher Preparation Notes for Spread of Infectious Disease and Population Growth." Provides background information for teachers to share with students regarding how easily infectious diseases spread.

Dole. Available online. URL: http://www.dole.com/#/home. Accessed July 25, 2010. From the fruit-growing company Dole, this Web site includes an area dedicated to teaching students how to make healthy choices.

Education World. Available online. URL: http: //www.educationworld.com. Accessed May 5, 2010. Contains lessons and links for teachers to use with students.

GlaxoSmithKline. "Welcome to Depression." Available online. URL: http://www.depression.com/. Accessed July 29, 2010. Web site from a pharmaceutical manufacturer that describes the symptoms of depression.

GRACE. Available online. URL: http://www.gracegrapevine.org/clinic.aspx. Accessed July 25, 2010. This is the official Web site of a non-profit agency specializing in offering help to families who have been affected by a current emergency and need assistance with clothing, food, financial, or health.

Gwinnet County School System. "Nutrition Education." Available online. URL: http://www.gwinnett.k12.ga.us/gcsnp.nsf/pages/NutritionEducation0~Education. Accessed July 25, 2010. The Gwinnett County School System has created a Web site dedicated to educating teachers and students about nutrition that allows for an in-depth study of various topics related to overall nutritional health.

Health Corps. Available online. URL: http://www.healthcorps.net/. Accessed July 25, 2010. Founded by Dr. Mehmet Oz, this Web site focuses on health education.

Henry the Hand. Available online. URL: http://www.henrythehand.com/. Accessed July 25, 2010. A fun child-oriented Web site that teaches children proper hand-washing techniques to avoid the spread of infection.

Hotchalk Lesson Plans Page. Available online. URL: http: //www.lessonplanspage.com. Accessed May 5, 2010. Source for lesson plans and links for educators.

Katz, Lillian. "How Can We Strengthen Self-esteem?" Available online. URL: http://www.kidsource.com/kidsource/content2/strengthen_children_self.html. Article written by the director of the ERIC Clearinghouse on elementary and early childhood education that explains what self-esteem is and the importance of positive self-esteem for children.

Kids Games. Available online. URL: http://www.gameskidsplay.net/. Accessed July 25, 2010. Web site with suggestions and rules for outdoor games that children can play to keep them active and healthy.

Kids.gov. Available online. URL: http://kids.gov/. Accessed July 25, 2010. Provides a variety of health information for and about children and includes a variety of games and exercises to help children become more active and healthy.

Kidshealth.org. Available online. URL: http://kidshealth.org/. Accessed July 25, 2010. This is an interactive and eye-catching site for kids, parents, and teens about health.

Mad Sci Network. Available online. URL: http: //www.madsci.org. Accessed May 5, 2010. Contains lessons and links for educators on science topics.

National Institute of Mental Health. "Eating Disorders." Available online. URL: http://www.nimh.nih.gov/health/publications/eating-disorders/complete-index.shtml. Accessed July 25, 2010. This Web site gives a description of what an eating disorder is, the different types of eating disorders, possible reasons why someone may have an eating disorder, and the damage that eating disorders can do to the body.

Net Doctor. Available online. URL: http://www.netdoctor.co.uk/teenagehealth/index.shtml. Accessed July 25, 2010. This Web site is dedicated to teenage health. Everything from drug abuse, eating healthy, exercise, puberty, skin problems, and well-being are covered on this Web site.

Nutrition Explorations. Available online. URL: http://www.nutritionexplorations.org/. Accessed July 25, 2010. This site can be used as a primary source for students learning about healthy eating and nutrition.

Parent Further. Available online. URL: http://www.parentfurther.com/. Accessed July 25, 2010. The Web site provides encouragement, advice, and tips for parents regarding raising healthy, successful, and self-sufficient individuals

Partnership for a Drug-Free America. "Tobacco." Available online. URL: http: //www.drugfree.org/Portal/drug_guide/Tobacco. Accessed May 5, 2010. Site provides detailed information about what tobacco is, what chemicals are found in tobacco, and the negative effects on health caused by tobacco.

PBS Kids. Available online. URL: http://pbskids.org/. Accessed July 25, 2010. Provides health-related educational activities and games for students.

The President's Challenge. Available online. URL: http://www.presidentschallenge. org/. Accessed July 25, 2010. This Web site offers children the ability to research their own health, set their own fitness goals, and learn about how to live a healthy lifestyle both in and out of school.

Princeton University. "Blood Pressure." Available online. URL: http: //wordnetweb. princeton.edu/perl/webwn?s=blood%20pressure. Accessed May 5, 2010. Defines blood pressure and explains how it is measured.

ScienceFairProjects411. Available online. URL: http: //www.sciencefairprojects411. com. Accessed May 5, 2010. Site that provides science-fair topic ideas.

Sciencenetlinks.com. Available online. URL: http: //www.sciencenetlinks.com. Accessed May 5, 2010. Site with links for educators regarding science topics.

Sparky the Fire Dog. Available online. URL: http://www.sparky.org/#/Sparky. Accessed July 25, 2010. This is a Web site with information and activities teaching children about fire safety, including an escape plan grid and safety checklist.

Stewart, David. "B.A.C. to the Future." Available online. URL: http: //www2.gsu.edu/ ~wwwche/mlessons.htm. Accessed May 5, 2010. Lesson about blood alcohol content.

Tutorials.com. "Learn 2 Take a Pulse." Available online. URL: http: //www.tutorials. com/09/0902/0902.asp. Accessed May 5, 2010. Explains how to find and count a person's pulse rate.

United States Department of Agriculture. Available online. URL: http: //www.usda.gov/ wps/portal/usdahome. Accessed May 5, 2010. Lesson plans created by the Trumball County Health Department for use in schools to prevent tobacco use.

USDA. "Healthier U.S. School Challenge." Available online. URL: http://teamnutrition. usda.gov/healthierUS/index.html. Accessed July 25, 2010. Team nutrition is a government Web site that encourages schools to become a part of a wellness team to get students healthy.

———. "My Pyramid." Available online. URL: http://www.mypyramid.gov/. Accessed July 25, 2010. My Pyramid is a nutrition education Web site created by the United States Department of Agriculture with a variety of games, posters, tips, coloring pages, and worksheets for children.

WebMD. "Dental Health and Fluoride Treatment." Available online. URL: http: // www.webmd.com/oral-health/guide/fluoride-treatment. Accessed May 5, 2010. Has information about the benefits of using fluoride to protect teeth from decay.

World Health Organization. Available online. URL: www.who.int/school_youth_health/ en/. Accessed July 25, 2010. The main goal of this portion of the Web site is to inform students about promoting health among youths.

Index